Sexy Second Act

Sexy Second Act

How to Remodel Your Life with Passion, Purpose, and a Paycheck!®

Sue Koch

Copyright © 2016 by Sue Koch

All rights reserved. No part of this publication may be reproduced, stored in or introduced into a retrieval system, or transmitted, in any form, or by any means (electronic, mechanical, photocopying, recording or otherwise) without the prior written permission of the publisher. This book is sold subject to the condition that it shall not, by way of trade or otherwise, be lent, resold, hired out, or otherwise circulated without the publisher's prior consent in any form of binding or cover other than that in which it is published and without a similar condition including this condition being imposed on the subsequent purchaser.

Book Cover Design: Marla Thompson
Editor: Eve Gumpel
Proofreader: Deb Coman
Typeset: Greg Salisbury
Portrait Photographer: Linda Joseph-Turek of Silver Moon Photography

DISCLAIMER: Readers of this publication agree that neither Sue Koch, nor her publisher will be held responsible or liable for damages that may be alleged as resulting directly or indirectly from the use of this publication. Neither the publisher nor the author can be held accountable for the information provided by, or actions, resulting from, accessing these resources.

This book is dedicated to my Badass Mastermind Group, whose members inspired, encouraged and supported me, and most of all, challenged me to stop *dreaming* about writing this book and just *do it*! I am forever grateful for their friendship, straight feedback, and kick-in-the-ass accountability throughout this journey.

Testimonials

Whether you are remodeling or renovating your life, read this book. Master Builder Sue Koch shares with you how to use building block words and phrases creatively to build your custom-designed life.

John Kurth
Author of *What are Your Words Wearing? How to Make Your Sales Communications Comprehensive, Substantial, and Precise.*

Sue leads you to experience a juicy and wow-filled second act as you move through new chapters of your life. If you've experienced discouragement or setbacks that interfere with reaching your dreams and goals, then you are sure to be inspired by this slightly funny and truly exhilarating book that will guide you to becoming unstoppable, regain your passion, confidence . . . and yep, your "sexy!"

Claudia Cooley
CEO of Claudia Cooley, Inc., a professional success and life enrichment coaching company, host of Rev Up for Success Radio, keynote speaker, and three time award winning and best-selling author of the *Rev Up for Success Series*.

Sue Koch is passionate about helping others find their passion, and often that is exactly what we need as we transition into our second act of life. This book brings an A to Z awareness to small things that can have a big impact.

Susan Sherbert
Author of A *White Hat and Rose Colored Glasses*

Acknowledgements

I want to acknowledge the people I look up to and admire. Each of them has qualities I aspire to expand in my own life. This book would not exist without their inspiration, courage, creativity, contribution, and passion.

Clients – Past, Present, and Future. You may learn from me, but I learn so much from you about dreaming, risk, courage, trust, joy, and more. You touch my heart and inspire me to keep growing.

Cindy Johnson – Sista-Friend, Coach and Trainer. Thanks for teaching me how to shine light into life's darkest corners to face what you don't want to face with quiet courage, gentleness, and grace.

Jarrett Gucci – Webmaster King. Thanks for always inspiring and challenging me to grow my technology skills and for constantly reminding me about the importance of staying playful, creative, and outside the box.

Karen Schmedeke – Creative Director, Coach, and Sista-Friend. Thanks for always believing in me and listening to my bullshit without judgment and with an open heart.

Kathy Lalonde – Retired teacher and former Self-Expression and Leadership Program Leader at Landmark Worldwide. Thanks for being a Sista-Friend who taught me about Community—how to create it, how to honor it, and how to show up for others from a place of love and commitment. Most of all, thanks for teaching me to never, ever give up on people.

Kelly Weppler-Hernandez – Energizer Bunny Marketing Master, Mentor, and friend. Thanks for being a role model who keeps going and going and going … and growing and growing and growing. You inspire me to do the same. I love your brilliance at helping people make sense of the marketing jungle.

Laura Neubauer – Thanks for being my Super Hero Badass Multipreneur friend and ally. I love your heart for helping others, for doing business inside of impeccable integrity, and for always playing "win-win."

Michael Boys – Rock-Solid Technical Titan and friend. It's been a joy to watch you grow your business step-by-grounded-step. You are always a dependable smile.

Teri Ritchie – Transformation Coach and Sista-Friend. Thanks for helping me put years of "woe is me" victimhood behind me to finally embrace my own Beautiful Badass Self.

Business Network International (BNI) – An amazingly talented group of business networkers, all of whom generously share their talent, expertise, and referral resources to help each other grow their businesses. The wonderful and enriching friendships and business relationships that have grown from my BNI membership are a delightfully unexpected, and very much appreciated, bonus.

Landmark Worldwide – Thanks for giving me the building blocks that started my journey to living my own "Sexy Second Act" and for the amazing community of remarkable people I've had the privilege to meet and grow with.

Innumerable Friends and Associates – Each of you has contributed to getting me to where I am today. If I missed mentioning you specifically, please know that I carry you in my heart. Without you, I would not be who I am, doing what I am doing—and loving it. You each have my eternal love and gratitude.

Contents

Disclaimer IV
Dedication V
Testimonials VII
Acknowledgements IX

How It Began 1
Why Second Act? 2
Why "Sexy"? 5
The Experiment 7
How Do Words Create Your World? 10
Believe It or Not, You Can "Nail" Your Sexy Second Act! ... 18
Intention 21
How to Play with This Book 23

A is for.. 27
Acknowledgement 28
Anger 30
Attitude 33
Awareness 34
"A" Remodeling Techniques 37

B is for… 39
Badass/Badassitude/Badassmanship 40
Bodacious 42
Bullshit 43
Buzzword 45
"B" Remodeling Techniques 47

C is for.. 49
Champion 50

Chaos 51
Chocolate 53
Commitment 54
Community 57
Congruence 59
"C" Remodeling Techniques 61

D is for. 63
Dance 64
Declaration 66
Desire 68
"D" Remodeling Techniques 70

E is for… 71
Embrace 72
Enlightenment 73
Epiphany 76
Excellence 77
"E" Remodeling Techniques 79

F is for… 81
Failure 82
Fierce 84
Focus 86
"F" Remodeling Techniques 87

G is for… 89
Gap 90
Generosity 94
Goals 96
Growth 98
"G" Remodeling Techniques 100

H is for…	101
Heart	102
Heaven	104
Hustle	105
"H" Remodeling Techniques	107
I is for…	109
Idea	110
Integrety	112
Intention	115
"I" Remodeling Techniques	117
J is for…	119
Jello	120
Jettison the Junk	121
Journey	123
Joy	125
Jump	126
"J" Remodeling Techniques	128
K is for…	129
Kaleidoscope	130
K.I.S.S.	132
"K" Remodeling Techniques	133
L is for…	135
Laughter	136
Leap of Faith	138
Legacy	141
Listening	143
"L" Remodeling Techniques	145

M is for…	147
Mastermind	148
Miracle	150
Money	152
"M" Remodeling Techniques	155
N is for…	157
No	158
Nothing	160
"N" Remodeling Techniques	162
O is for…	163
Observer	164
One	166
Orgasm	168
"O" Remodeling Techniques	169
P is for…	171
Passion	172
Play	174
Purpose	176
"P" Remodeling Techniques	178
Q is for…	179
Quality Questions	180
Quiet	182
Quit	184
"Q" Remodeling Techniques	185
R is for…	187
Renegade	188

Responsibility	190
Rigor	192
"R" Remodeling Techniques	194
S is for…	195
Serendipity	196
Sexy	198
So What?	200
Surrender	202
"S" Remodeling Techniques	204
T is for…	205
Transition	206
Trust	209
Truth	211
"T" Remodeling Techniques	213
U is for…	215
Unreasonable	216
Uplift	218
"U" Remodeling Techniques	220
V is for…	221
Values	222
Vibration	224
Vivid Vision	226
"V" Remodeling Techniques	228
W is for…	229
Who	230
Wisdom	232
"W" Remodeling Techniques	234

X is for…	235
X-Ray Vision	236
"X" Remodeling Techniques	238
Y is for…	239
Year	240
YOLO – You Only Live Once	242
Yum	244
"Y" Remodeling Techniques	245
Z is for…	247
Zero	248
Zigzag	250
"Z" Remodeling Techniques	251
Final Thoughts	252
Author Biography	253
Designing Your Sexy Second Act?	255

How It Began

The idea for this book was born one day as I meandered through a quaint beachside gift shop in Laguna Beach, California. I spotted a plaque that listed twenty-six inspiring words and phrases, one for each letter of the alphabet. The plaque appealed to my love of words. I had to buy it.

Each morning thereafter, as I sipped my cup of English breakfast tea, I thought about the plaque's words and phrases. I found myself mentally creating my own inspirational word list, which eventually triggered an "aha" moment.

Why not write a book, using my favorite words and phrases, to encourage others who are ready to remodel and design a Sexy Second Act career or life?

I'd been wanting to write a book for years. Now I had a topic, born out of my desire to inspire people who aren't sure how to go about remodeling a life that has gotten stale or that no longer fits who they are.

This book contains a collection of my favorite building block words and phrases from A to Z. My word choices include my personal interpretations. You are not stuck with them. Use the ones you like. Toss the ones you don't. Create your own interpretations. Add your own words. Borrow from my list to start creating your own building block vocabulary.

Use your power word building blocks to jumpstart you on your path to becoming the Master Builder of a juicy, wow-filled, Sexy Second Act. What could be more fun than "nailing" a career and life that include passion, purpose, and contribution? And yes ... let's not forget ... *a paycheck*!

Why Second Act?

After I was let go from my corporate job in 2002, I started reading, thinking, and soul-searching about what it takes to successfully navigate a major career or life transition, particularly in the second half of life.

The world is changing so fast that we can no longer depend on what worked in the past. Many doors have closed, or are closing, as industries downsize or send repeatable work overseas. Not only that, technology is rapidly changing the landscape of how we live and where we work.

Even a single life change can be challenging. With every part of our lives turning upside down, it's no wonder many of us feel like we are standing on a shaky foundation.

I was curious about how other baby boomers were dealing with these changes:

- Were they grappling with the same issues as I was?
- Were they wondering how to do work that mattered and still make a living?
- Were they questioning whether retirement was even an option?
- Did they still have too much energy and too many good years left to spend them sitting on the sidelines?
- If downsized industries and ageism kept them from finding jobs, what alternatives were they discovering?

My research introduced me to terms I'd never heard of, like "Encore Career," "Second Act," and "Slash Career." Of all the terms I learned, I like "Second Act" best. It falls most closely in line with what my clients tell me they want.

A Second Act isn't about coming back onstage to do more of what you've already done. A Second Act is designed to further the play called "Your Life," by expressing yourself, playfully and passionately, through your work. It's designing work in a way you haven't been able to design it before, and doing it in a way that fulfills and pays you.

Why Second Act

Werner Erhard, teacher, consultant, and creator of "est" (Erhard Seminars Training), describes a Second Act using the metaphor of a three-act play:

- Act I represents your past and includes everything you know, believe, or have experienced up to now. You can draw upon the information and your experiences, but you cannot change anything, since Act I is finished.
- Act II includes what you are experiencing now. It includes only what is occurring in the present moment. Act II functions as a bridge between what happened in Act I and the beginning of Act III. Act II is where you have the ability to make choices. You can't choose in Act I because it's done. You can't choose in Act III because it hasn't occurred yet.
- Act III represents your future. The script you design for Act III influences and guides the actions you take in Act II. To bring about the future you want in Act III, you must be willing to make conscious choices and be responsible for them right now, in Act II.

The most powerful part of this metaphor is that you never get to Act III. You are always living in Act II.

Designing your life as if it was a three-act play is exciting! It means you are never stuck with the script you've got. In every moment, you have the ability to rewrite your Second Act to align with how you want Act III to go.

Doesn't that make the idea of a "Second Act" career or life sound way, way cool? The ability to redesign your career and life-building blueprint takes you out of being stuck with a "prefabricated" one. It puts you into a custom-designed career and life of your own making.

You get to choose how and where to place each building block in a way that's unique to you. How fun would it be to design your Sexy Second Act life and career to be an ongoing, exhilarating, moment-by-moment, malleable creation?

How does purpose fit into this picture? In all my years as a coach, I've never had a client tell me they didn't care about making a difference. If that is true for you, then my next question is: How?

That question generally brings a "deer-in-the-headlights" expression to the faces of my clients. I can almost hear them thinking, "If I knew the answer to that question, I wouldn't need you!"

The answer is simple, even though it isn't necessarily easy. What you love—what you are passionate about—is the means by which you are meant to make a difference. The things you love are your personal building blocks for designing a life of purpose.

Oh yeah, I know what you are thinking. There's no way you can possibly tie your purpose into your burning desire to live on a tropical island in your swimsuit, or sail around the world on a yacht, or raise llamas in Tibet. Not only that, you are probably thinking there's no way to make a living doing what you love.

Not so fast. Don't bet on that notion just yet.

For one thing, beyond taking care of the basics, money may, or may not, be a mandatory or motivational "paycheck" for you. You may be fulfilled by other rewards, like contribution, creativity, or self-expression.

For another, where one door closes, another one opens. Technology is opening up far-reaching opportunities we have barely begun to explore.

The blueprint for how you put your career and life of Passion, Purpose, and a Paycheck® together in Act II is completely up to you. You are only limited by your desire, imagination, and willingness to put on your work pants and boots, grab your tools, and get to work.

Why "Sexy" ?

The short—and perhaps glib—answer is ... why not?

If clothing and housing styles get stale and go out of fashion, then doesn't it stand to reason that careers and lifestyles become passé, too? You are not who you were five, ten, twenty years ago or more. A lifestyle or career remodel may be exactly what you need to rekindle the heat of your sexy, inner fire. And as long as you are alive and healthy, there is no reason for you to stop stoking that fire.

Your life isn't over. Your Sexy Second Act may signal the beginning of your real life—the one you would have designed to fit you perfectly a long time ago, if you had only known better.

Like a "loved-in" house, you have great bones. A bit of sprucing up may be all you need to blossom into the full glory of the sexy, badass, living-full-out human being you were put on the planet to become.

No matter what age you are, living your life in a way that matters to you, makes you attractive and sexy. When you feel attractive and sexy, you become a magnet for drawing amazing people, opportunities, and experiences to you.

Think about a time when you found the perfect-fit-for-you outfit. You tried it on and you felt like a stud or a goddess, didn't you?

You stood up tall. Your eyes gleamed. You walked differently. You moved with confidence, grace and ease.

Your confidence turned heads. Everyone you encountered wanted to be around you. You felt sexy!

That's what happens when you wear a career and life that fit you like a velvet glove. Each day feels magical. You look and feel younger. You overflow with anticipation and vitality. You have a bounce in your step.

You're engaged and excited. You are having so much fun, people are attracted to you and to the work you are doing. They want to jump into your life or career game with you, bringing their passion, talents and resources along with them, stoking your fire and making it burn even hotter.

So, if you are experiencing feelings of discontent, boredom, or frustration, don't ignore them. Don't decide something is wrong and give up.

Embrace your discontent and boredom. Treat them as loving signals from your Higher Self that it's time for a life-stage makeover. It's time to do the demolition work needed to make way for a brand new design.

Yeah, I know. Going through a remodel can be daunting, unsettling, and downright messy and dirty. But if you've ever gone through one, you know you'll end up with something beautiful on the other side. That makes every bit of chaos worth it.

When you surrender to doing something stimulating and meaningful, when you pour your heart and soul into it, you become unstoppable, powerful, confident ... and yep ... sexy! Who doesn't want more of feeling like that?

The Experiment

For the most part, we humans are careless with our language. We rarely stop to reflect upon what we say, how we say it, or how it impacts us and others.

Think about the words you use daily. Are they potent? Do you feel powerful and confident when you speak? Is your voice strong?

If you were to listen to yourself speaking, what would you hear? Would you tolerate it if another person spoke to you the way you speak to yourself?

What do the people you care about hear when you speak to them? Do they feel uplifted and supported? Or do they feel de-energized and unappreciated?

Building a house requires you to use strong, solid materials in creative ways. Building your Sexy Second Act requires you to use strong, solid language in creative ways. You start by remodeling the words you use when you talk to yourself, and then you remodel the way you communicate with others.

In construction, carelessness is a major factor in accidents where people get physically hurt or killed. Careless communication is just as dangerous, because it spiritually hurts, maims, and kills. Careless communication results in destructive interactions and behavior, which lead to poor and undesirable outcomes.

Careless communication leaves you with messes to clean up—if you even bother to take responsibility for repairing the damage. In my experience, people generally don't clean up the communication messes they make. They "hit and run" or they sweep the mess under the rug. Out of embarrassment or fear, they pretend the mess didn't happen, or that someone else is responsible.

You can ignore the messes you make, but you can't get rid of them. They accumulate and turn into smelly, energy-draining drama and turmoil.

Ignoring them long enough can cause them to morph into physical illness. The impact of messy communication can last decades or, in the worst-case scenario, a lifetime!

Messes weigh you down. Cleaning them up is like opening all the doors and windows on a bright, spring day. The influx of fresh air cleans out the stale air, refreshes you, and frees you up to focus on taking care of stuff that matters to you.

What kind of stuff, you ask? Here are a few suggestions to ponder, just for starters: you could grow green things, or wild things, or weird things. You could paint trees, hike the John Muir Trail, or jump from the edge of space. You could knit skull caps, run marathons, or sail around the world on a surfboard. You could flip a house, climb Mount Everest, or run away and join the circus. You could rescue pit bulls, sculpt ice statues, or write the Great American Novel. You could feed the hungry, raise orphans, save rain forests, or start a business in your garage.

The list of things you could do is limited only by your desire, your imagination, and your willingness to dive in and go for it, full-tilt boogie. In his book, *Above All Else: A World Champion Skydiver's Story of Survival and What It Taught Him About Fear, Adversity, and Success* (Skyhorse Publishing, 2011), champion skydiver Dan Brodsky-Chenfeld offers this criteria for going after a Big, Juicy Goal:

- Do I believe it's possible to succeed?
- Do I want it badly enough to do what it's going to take to make it happen?

If you want it, if it's possible, and if you are willing to do what it takes, somebody is meant to benefit from it! The things you are passionate about are meant to be joyful for you and of service to others.

Accomplishing the goals that truly matter to you begins with remodeling your language—especially the way you talk to yourself. It's the surest way I know of to begin remodeling your life! When you redesign your interior world by changing how you speak to yourself, your exterior world takes care of itself.

This book is designed to be used as your mini-lab "word and energy" experiment. You might say it contains "language Legos®" for you to use as building blocks to replace your mental blocks.

You'll have an opportunity to examine the life you built in Act I with your words. You'll see how your language impacts the daily choices you make in Act II.

You'll get to look at which "rooms" in your life you want to beautify and make delightfully functional by demolishing outmoded ways of thinking and speaking that weaken your foundation. You'll start building a new bridge to Act III from a strong foundation.

Choose words that help you construct a sexy life of ecstasy, power and freedom. Join what I like to call the ranks of God's mini-me "Masters of Manifestation" in training.

How Do Words Create Your World?

Who in the world came up with the notion that words can never hurt you? We inflict terrible and painful wounds on ourselves and on each other with our words—wounds that leave deep and permanent scars. Wounds that hurt as much, or more, than sticks or stones ever could.

Sticks and stones may kill your body. Words can kill your spirit.

Let's stop verbally wounding and killing ourselves and each other. Let's support each other to design blow-out-the-walls, bodaciously badass, amazingly love-filled Sexy Second Act lives and careers.

I want you to feel that being alive to experience your challenges, defeats, joy, love, and victory celebrations is the most miraculous gift you've ever been given. I want you to experience that gift in every cell of your body.

What would it feel like to intentionally stop yourself from speaking destructive words associated with jealousy, fear, hate, suffering, anger, or sorrow? How would that change your life?

What would it feel like to intentionally speak every word in every moment to everyone, including yourself, as if you were having a love affair? What would it feel like to hear only divinely loving words in your ears?

Can you imagine your life becoming anything other than an amazingly ecstatic, healthy, sexy-passionate, "love-gasmic" experience?

If your life isn't burning red-hot like that most of the time; if you aren't clicking along on all cylinders at close to a "ten"; if your inner fire has cooled into lukewarm embers—isn't it time to remodel? Isn't it time to:

- Turn up the heat?
- Crank up the thermostat on your joy scale to a fun-tastically "hot" temperature?
- Light up the world with the glow of your inner flame?

If you are feeling skeptical; if you think this seems "effing" impossible; I

How Do Words Create Your World?

completely get it. I've been there.

At a subconscious level, I decided at a fairly early age that something was wrong with me; that I didn't fit in; and that I probably never would. I felt like the best I could do was "get by."

From then on, the jig was up. You can't design and build a "sexy" life on a foundation of "get-by" language. My inner programming went like this:

- Don't take risks.
- Don't be seen.
- Don't make waves.
- Don't try too hard.
- Don't let 'em see your flaws.

The outward manifestation of my "get-by" language was that I held myself back. I deliberately did my best to fly under the radar. I avoided attempting anything new if I didn't know for sure, ahead of time, that I could accomplish it.

I remember thinking, "Why bother? It'll never work out anyhow," when faced with something challenging and new. I defeated myself before I started.

Over the years, my life shrank to a minuscule and unworkable size. I felt lonely and sad. Worst of all, I felt helpless to change anything.

If "Whoever Was In Charge" had decided it was my time to go, I would have been OK with that. Woe was me.

I made myself miserable shedding bitter tears of self-pity and sadness. I felt as if I'd missed out on something I thought everyone else knew except me—the "secret" to living a joy-filled life.

Can you guess what kind of results my "get-by" language produced? Yep. "Get-by" results. You can imagine how sexy and fun it was living that life.

My unhappiness didn't stem from outward circumstances. It came from poor interior design—a life built on a foundation of lousy internal dialogue about what I believed to be true about me and about life.

I admired others for doing things I didn't have the courage to do, but I couldn't imagine living a courageous life. I couldn't imagine shedding tears of joy and gratitude merely by having the opportunity to wake up and fill each day with fun, adventure, and contribution.

Don't get me wrong. By most standards, I led a pretty good life. I was blessed with dedicated and loving parents. I experienced a pretty typical childhood in a normally dysfunctional family. I say "normally dysfunctional" because I believe almost every family is dysfunctional to one degree or another.

After high school graduation, I attended trade school classes rather than enroll in college. I thought I was "too dumb" to get a higher education.

I tried a couple of jobs before finally landing one that "stuck"—in the engineering and construction industry. It was a great job with good people, but it wasn't my dream job. I had no idea what my dream job was.

Nonetheless, I worked hard. I wanted to better myself. I learned, and eventually got promoted to an interesting job at a salary level that afforded me the opportunity to do many things I enjoyed doing.

From the outside looking in, I suspect my life looked pretty dang good. From the inside looking out? Not so much.

It didn't matter how good I was at my job or what accolades I received. The committee in my head kept telling me what a fraud I was. It yelled at me so loudly, I couldn't hear the good stuff. I missed out on a ton of joy.

I didn't have the tools to tell the committee to shut the hell up. The noise was so persistent, I could barely catch more than a glimpse now and then of how achingly delicious, magnificent, and over-the-top fantastic it is just to have been given the gift of life!

I couldn't fathom what a miracle it was to be alive against the staggering odds of even being born. I couldn't see how absolutely incredible it was to get to "play" for even a short while on this beautiful, insignificant, pale blue marble, spinning crazily around the Milky Way galaxy in some obscure little corner of the universe.

What finally happened to shift my awareness from despair to happiness? I hit bottom, emotionally. I finally wore myself out from suppressing who I was and keeping myself uptight and in control.

I didn't know it then, but reaching the point of emotional exhaustion was a gift. I finally had to let go of holding back, making myself invisible, and "getting by." I no longer had the energy to play that game.

There's a lot to be said for surrendering what isn't working in your life to your Higher Power. I highly recommend it. My experience is that when you do, Serendipity shows up, wearing sexy shoes and an impish smile.

Serendipity sashayed into my life in the form of a friend who, seemingly out of the blue, invited me to attend an introduction to a personal growth course. What I heard during the presentation woke me up. It both excited and terrified me.

I knew that if I chose to participate, I could no longer hide out or fly under the radar. Even though it was scary, I knew it was exactly what I needed.

The program jumpstarted my interior design remodel. I had no choice but to demolish many things I had believed and told myself about who I was and what life was. I realized that while I had lots of compassion for others, I was brutally—and I do mean "brutally"—biased and misguided in my viewpoint about me.

For the first time, I listened to—and questioned—what the committee in my head told me was the "truth" about who I was. You know that committee. It's the voices of parents, teachers, and other caregivers who meant well, but who didn't always speak in a loving and supportive way. The language you hear in your formative years sticks with you as "truth."

Observing those voices, rather than listening to them, helped me discover how dead wrong I was about my view of myself and the world. The course gave me the tools I needed to demolish my outdated and unworkable model of thinking and speaking.

Slowly, I began to fabricate and build a bridge to a new Act III, using a well-designed model of language. Getting through the renovation was tough.

When you remodel, you see stuff hidden behind the walls you didn't know was there. Not all of it was pretty, but I learned to accept and embrace all the facets of myself—the good, the bad, and the ugly.

You see, the good, the bad, and the ugly are all part of the wiring inside the structural design we call "human being." Recognizing that it's not personal, it's just part of our design, gave me permission to relax.

I learned to laugh at how funny—and tragic—it is that we humans run around wasting energy and acting like we have it all together when the reality is that most of us don't have a clue. Hiding our cluelessness is killing us. It's time to let the cat out of the bag, tell the truth, and build a new, workable and loving model of language.

The truth is that nobody has it together. We screw up. We are often unkind and mean. We are not always good, compassionate, or loving. We get angry and hurt, and that causes us to react out of malice and jealousy. We get scared and run. We often play smaller than we are capable of playing.

When I saw the good, bad, and ugly in myself, I was able to open up, get real, and let go of pretending or trying to hide my flaws. As a result, I started to see my gifts more clearly—my loyalty, my sense of humor, my intelligence, my love for people, my bulldog persistence, and my creativity.

I discovered that I want life to be a party. I want everyone to join the fun by designing and building a Second Act life and career that feels sexy, vibrant, and alive!

Following that discovery, my first question was—how the heck do I do this?

Can you hear my outmoded language pattern and theme trying to sneak back in? Almost immediately, the committee in my head began yelling: "Don't try; it'll never work out. You're too dumb. You'll fail. You'll never pull that game off in a million years."

By now I was learning to quiet those voices down to a whisper. A new voice began chiming in. It was the voice of possibility.

Slowly, I came to I realize that, by golly, there is a secret to living a joy-filled life. The secret is to invent a mind-boggling, big, bodaciously badass life game to play that's crazy fun and fulfills your purpose.

My invitation to you, through this book, is to invent a bodacious life game big enough to shut the committee up. Invent a game big enough to shift your monkey-mind's attention to solving sexy, juicy problems and away from inventing petty ones.

The naysayer committee in your head doesn't have a chance against a big, juicy life game. It has no choice but to head for the hills.

I chose coaching as the vehicle for playing my life game and fulfilling my mission to "powerfully, passionately, and purposefully celebrate life." My desire, intention, and commitment to help my clients design and build a Sexy Second Act was another call for Serendipity—God love her—to saunter sassily back into my life.

She beckoned me, waving that saucy finger of hers, urging me to trust and follow my own heart. The more I did, the more comfortable I felt in my own skin.

My anxiety all but disappeared. The icy, cold place I had always felt in the center of my chest, thawed out. I could feel myself opening up to take bigger risks, to try things I wasn't sure I'd succeed at, and to let my authentic self be seen.

Language is the ultimate art of creation. Without it, we wouldn't be human. Witnessing the power of language to transform is endlessly fascinating. The mind is so potent! In its misguided mission to protect us, it covers up and denies what our hearts know to be true.

It is astonishing how quickly someone's aliveness is squashed by words like "practical" and "safe," and how quickly energy is restored by words like "ecstasy," "love," and "play."

It's stunning to observe people instantly age when they talk about problems and what they perceive to be unworkable and hopeless circumstances. But when they speak about what brings them "passion," "freedom," and "joy," they drop ten or fifteen years in age—or more—in a heartbeat.

Here's a notion that might scare the crap out of you: you are designed to move, grow, expand, widen your horizons, and experience life fully—not safely. After a lifetime of playing it safe and hiding your true colors, you might be wondering how in the world you learn to take a chance on living a life of balls-out joy and vitality.

It's simple. You choose it.

Simple doesn't mean easy. The committee of demons in your head will resist. In his book, *Do the Work* (The Domino Project, 2011, p. 9), Steven Pressfield nails it when he talks about resistance. He says: "Resistance plays for keeps. Resistance's goal is not to wound or disable ... Resistance aims to kill."

So how do you keep a tough enemy like resistance from killing your dreams?

You look for the gift wrapped up inside the curse. The gift of resistance is that it can be a powerful sculpting tool. Use it to chip away at the mucky, sucky, yucky language you've wrapped yourself up in your whole life without even knowing it. Keep chipping and sculpting until the true you shines through.

Use this book as your ally to help you demolish your resistance. Use it as a resource to help you create your own special blueprint for building a bridge to your custom-made, one-of-a-kind Act III. Adopt powerful Act II language that opens up exciting possibilities for your Sexy Second Act career and life! Allow the message within these pages to help you:

- Pay attention to your current language.
- Feel the energy of your words in your body.
- Distinguish between what you think you want and what you truly and authentically want.
- Start speaking and manifesting what you authentically want into your experience.
- See what a trickster the committee in your head is when it tells you your dreams are too big, you're too small—and besides, it's way too risky!
- Quiet the voices of the committee to finally hear the dreams of your heart.

You have only one job. Do what calls to your heart. Quit judging its worthiness, or yours. Do it and let go of the outcome.

It all comes down to choosing. Choose to keep things the way they are or choose to change them up. I hope you'll choose to demolish your old model of language and build a bridge that connects you to the language of your heart, which is the only language worth listening to.

Believe It or Not, You Can "Nail" Your Sexy Second Act!

Do you find it annoying when successful people say, "If I can do it, you can do it"? Yeah, right.

I saw "successful people" as having money up the wazoo, enjoying big, fancy houses, traveling everywhere, hobnobbing with famous people, and living in the lap of luxury. No way could I be successful.

Or so I thought.

I thought they had some "it" quality that set them apart ... a quality I lacked and could never attain. Or else they were just born under some lucky star.

I was half right. Truly successful people did have something I lacked. That something was belief—they believed in themselves in ways I didn't believe in me. My inner dialogue told me that weird karma or some other Unknown Force was standing between me and the key that could unlock the door to the successful life I yearned for.

My inner world was overcrowded with limiting beliefs and fear. I built a narrow, cramped "box" for myself with little room to breathe. I felt like I would suffocate if I didn't get out.

Thank goodness I discovered an escape hatch before my oxygen ran out.

My Purpose.

Purpose was the siren song that lured me out of my box. Purpose gave me the courage to cut myself some slack and appreciate who I was just as I was—and how I am today, in Act II.

Purpose gets me out of bed out every day. Purpose helps me stay true to what I believe I came here to do.

Purpose will do that for you, too. Purpose compels you to build an Act III that's worthy of your time, energy, spirit, heart and skills. It moves you beyond who you know yourself to be to become a bigger, badassier, bolder, stronger, and happier you than you ever dreamed possible. But, let me share a secret with you: Purpose isn't a cure-all or "magic bullet." Purpose won't "fix" you or your life.

That's the bad news.

The good news is that you don't need fixing.

You'll still make messes. But you will be less willing to sweep them under the carpet. You will want to clean them up quickly, but out in the open rather than secretly. You'll be too busy honoring your purpose to allow messes to trip you up for long.

You'll have to watch out for traps. The committee loves setting them to keep you chained to "the way you are" or "the way life is" or "the way it's always been."

Beware of thinking you'll permanently get your life cleaned up and shiny and all your neat little rows organized, once and for all. You'll still have upsets. They might be external events like an earthquake or a tornado that turns your world upside down and sideways.

Or you might face a human-made event like a divorce, death of a loved one, life-threatening medical diagnosis, or job loss. What will you do then?:

- Accept that you are in the "demo" phase of a life stage, and a remodel is pending.
- Accept that your life may feel chaotic and look ugly for a while.
- Accept that you may not like what you discover behind the walls, but you can replace what isn't working with something that does.
- Give yourself permission to grieve. Or scream. Or get angry and hit something (but not someone!)
- Be patient until the dust settles, and then clear out the rubble.
- Put on your tool belt and get to work building something fresh, colorful, and new from the ground up.
- When all else fails, laugh at the divine insanity of being human.

Your Sexy Second Act is a DIY project. You'll have to design the blueprint. You can't depend on what you've known in the past. There's no precedent for the massive shifts and changes going on in today's world.

The bad news is that there are no guidelines for you to follow. The good news is that you get to make it up!

Here's what you don't do: You don't sit and ruminate about it; you don't try to figure it all out at once. You can't have it all figured out before you even start.

To nail it, start from where you are with what you've got. You'll find out that what you've got right now is enough ... more than enough ... to build the Sexy Second Act you were designed to live.

Trust your "design ideas," even if they don't make sense during the construction phase. Let yourself dance with nonsense and chaos. Throw paint at the walls. Build something and, if you hate it, demolish it and build something else.

Remember that language is your art and chaos is your friend; that knowledge will keep you sane in what appears to be an insane world. You may even discover perfection in the destruction of all that came before.

Learn to embrace the ultimate paradox—out of messiness and chaos emerge order, peace, and the scrumptious acceptance of life as it is and you as you are—messy and beautiful and divine and wonderful and crazy and downright "effing" weird.

My guess is you've been in houses that make you wonder how anyone could live there. The owners may love their home that's a crazy-quilt of colors or styles. It may make no sense to you that they are happy and thriving in a house that would drive you nuts.

In the same way, your life may never make sense to anyone else but you. So what? You, living your juiciest life is what matters. It's the only thing that matters.

You'll know you've nailed it when ... :

- You can embrace your life's beauty and elegant design.
- You find as much delight in the mess as you do in the beauty.
- Every day becomes a yummy adventure.
- You laugh out loud at the quirky gifts, messages, challenges, and funny little signals "Whoever Is In Charge" delivers to help you along your path to awareness of the only thing that really matters ... living a juicy, sexy life!
- You find ecstasy and fulfillment in contributing your gifts and skills to others—just because you can!

Intention

The intention of this book is to take a sassy and humorous look at life's craziness and chaos as the old systems we've lived with, and relied on for decades, crumble around us. Can you design and build a Sexy Second Act when the life you are living blows up on you or when you are ready to blow it up yourself?

You bet you can!

The book isn't about giving you answers. You already have them inside you. It just may take a little digging on your part to excavate them.

The words I chose and my thoughts about their meaning, combined with my sharing my life experience, are intended to assist you to think differently. Or better yet, how to think less and play more … with ways you can nail your über "badass" Sexy Second Act life or career, based on what's true for you deep down inside your heart of hearts.

It's about getting in touch with what you feel and learning to trust and love it. It's about learning what to give up worrying about and how to distinguish between what matters to you and what doesn't. And it's about learning to speak more often about things that matter.

And it's about how to stop taking your journey through this wild ride called "life" so gosh-darned seriously! As my friend Teri says, "Life is fatal, but it's not serious." It's much too amusement-park-fun-house-crazy a journey for serious!

So, why not find ways to embrace the wild, crazy and delicious mess that life is? Trust me—embracing wild-ass crazy is doable!

Embrace the idea that "Whoever Is In Charge" has a funky sense of humor. Perhaps the Divine One deliberately keeps us on our toes by constantly changing things up and putting us on paths that contain all sorts of weird, unexpected twists and wild, hairpin turns. It must be highly entertaining to watch how we humans deal with them.

I like to believe we inspire divine giggles of delight and surprise when we manage to pull off something really badass cool with the circumstances we are given! Otherwise, what the heck is the point?

The journey of life is endlessly fascinating. As John Lennon of the Beatles wrote in the lyrics of "Beautiful Boy (Darling Boy)": "Life is what happens to you while you're busy making other plans." Or as my friend Eve tells me, there's a Yiddish proverb that says "Man plans, God laughs."

The point is that, no matter how well we plan it, life has a way of throwing us off course. Or what we think is off course.

What if Life and the Universe know when it's time for us to grow? What if we're deliberately shaken up when it's time for us go in the direction we were meant to go in all along—in the direction of our highest soul development and purpose?

Once we start moving in that direction, even when we can't see the whole path, life gets simple, elegant, peaceful, rewarding and—best of all—fun! That's how we "know" from deep inside that we're in alignment with who we are meant to be and what we are meant to do.

So why not just throw your arms open wide and embrace it all, however it shows up? Embrace your mistakes. Embrace your flaws and weaknesses. Embrace your victories. Embrace what you can't control as well as what you can. Embrace it all, then let it go. Let it flow through your fingers like water.

How to Play with This Book

Dive into this book in the spirit in which it was written. Have fun. Don't work with this book. Play with it in any way your spirit moves you.

Your left brain may not like that. It may resist, doing its best to thwart you from having fun. It may tell you to get back to the "serious" business of survival.

Resistance will do its best to make you feel uncomfortable. That's OK. Your left brain is doing what it does best—cataloging and organizing everything you've learned and experienced into neat little rows.

When that happens, shout "leggo!" to your left brain, and scatter the pieces. Invite your creative right brain out to play. Do something different from what you are used to doing. Do it "messy" if you always do it "organized" and vice-versa.

Pick a random page or letter to read. Read the book backward if you always start on the first page. Read lying on the floor like a kid with your feet up on the furniture. Go outside and read while lying on the grass in the sun. Hang upside down from a tree branch.

However you choose to play will be perfect. Your creative right brain will love you for giving it the open space in which to breathe.

Trust your intuition to tell you how you play best. Here are a few suggestions if you can't break free of your habitual way of learning and doing:

- Start at the beginning and play your way through the entire alphabet from "A" to "Z." At the end of each chapter are suggested "remodeling techniques." Pick at least one that resonates with you and do it.
- Read the entire book in one sitting.
- Start at the end with the letter "Z" and play your way to "A."
- Start with "A" and play with the "A" words one day, the "B" words the next day, and so forth. Randomly pick one, two, or three words to play with throughout your day.
- Open a page, close your eyes, put your finger on a word and play with that word—or all the words starting with that letter.

- Start with the first letter of your first name and pick a word that starts with the same letter.
- Pick words that start with each letter of your first (or last) name and string them together. Who knows? You may get a message that makes perfect sense. Or not.
- Pick words that start with your spouse's first name or your kids' first names and string them together.
- Pick three random words from different parts of the book. After reading them, pick at least one "remodeling technique" to do.
- Play with a specific word (or words) for a day, a week, a month or a year.
- Close your eyes. Think about a situation where you are feeling "stuck." With your eyes still closed, allow the book to open to a random page and put your finger on a word. Play with how that word might lead you to a solution.

Are you getting the message?

There is no right way or wrong way to read this book. However you choose to play with it, is perfect. It's meant to be your resource. Use it to inspire you to begin designing your Bodaciously Badass Sexy Second Act.

You can even change it up from time to time. Play one way until you get bored and then choose a different way to play.

Playing with friends or associates in a reading group or mastermind group is the badassiest way to have fun. Groups get everyone's brain operating creatively in expanded ways.

Play with a group where everyone is committed to winning. The best results come when everyone is open to being led in the direction of fun, exciting, and expanded possibilities.

Your key to your success is to play full out, whichever way you choose to play. Don't settle for just reading the book and hoping for an "aha" or two. Mastery comes from practice:

How to Play with This Book

- Practice the "remodeling techniques" at the end of each chapter.
- Journal your thoughts.
- Make a pact with someone you trust to call you on your disempowering language when they hear it. Do the same for them.
- Notice changes in your energy—and the results you achieve in your life—as you remodel your language.
- Celebrate your victories!

Now that you've got the picture, let's begin! Ready ... set ... go!

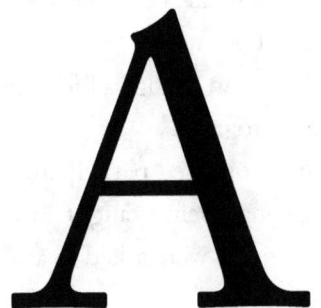

ACKNOWLEDGEMENT

We humans are downright miserly when it comes to offering acknowledgement. We are even stingier about letting it in.

How often do you send an email, text message, or invitation that is never acknowledged? How does that make you feel?

How often do you give a compliment, only to have it blown off? How often do you blow off or dismiss compliments given to you? Have you ever stopped to think about how that makes the other person feel?

We tend to think it takes doing something big to make a difference. As a result, we miss opportunities to make a difference every day for people we care about who are right in front of our noses.

A simple acknowledgement can change a life. I learned that beautiful lesson when I coached a leadership program.

This particular program encouraged participants to share as they grappled with integrating the distinctions being taught in the course. At the end of each person's share, all participants were asked to acknowledge the person who shared with applause.

This made the person who was sharing enormously uncomfortable at first. Very few participants could stand at ease and just take in acknowledgement without fidgeting and trying to "escape" back to their seats.

The course leader came up with a brilliant idea. She asked the "runaways" to come back to the front of the room. She asked them to stand still, look at their fellow participants, and "be with" the acknowledgement.

You'd think they were being asked to stand in front of a firing squad. They squirmed, blushed, looked down, or tried to do something funny—like make a face or bow dramatically—anything to avoid simply allowing the gift of acknowledgement to wash over them.

It took practice but, over time, the transformation was amazing to watch. Participants learned to relax, stop fidgeting, and make eye contact. They opened up to share authentically and vulnerably. They learned to stand peacefully, at ease in their power, and bask in the warm glow of acknowledgement.

ACKNOWLEDGEMENT

It was delicious to watch and delightful to hear their confidence grow out of that one practice. Their newfound confidence grew until it spilled over into all areas of their lives.

Acknowledgement—true, genuine, heartfelt acknowledgement—can soften the hardest heart. It opens the door to trust, intimacy, vulnerability, and community.

Are you someone who gives acknowledgement but deflects it when it's aimed at you? Stop shying away. Stop cheating yourself out of receiving the gift of acknowledgement. Be willing to receive as well as to give.

Energy has to flow in two directions to maintain balance. Don't block the flow by cheating the giver out of the opportunity to acknowledge you. Take it in with gratitude and humbly thank them for the gift.

Allow someone who cares about you to acknowledge you. Give it generously and receive it graciously. It's a gift on both sides.

ANGER

Anger ... the "A" word we don't like to look at.

Women especially are taught that it isn't "nice" or "ladylike" to express anger. So we learn to suppress it.

Suppressing anger doesn't make it go away. It simmers away inside, and the pressure keeps building and building until we can no longer ignore it.

If we do express it, it's likely to come out in slimy ways with troll-like posts, emails, or texts. Or we let it out overtly through bullying, put-downs, or terrorism.

When I took my first honest-to-goodness peek at my suppressed anger, it scared the hell out of me. If I didn't keep an extremely tight lid on it, I thought, it would explode out of me like an atom bomb, taking a whole bunch of people—maybe even the entire planet—with me. It seemed better to hide the angry volcano roiling inside me.

As I began to acknowledge the depth of my anger, I wrote a poem about it. Here's a portion of what I wrote:

> *A terrorist lives inside me, and she scares me half to death.*
> *A terrorist lives inside me, and I've denied her with every breath.*
> *A terrorist lives inside me, and I do not want to know her.*
> *A terrorist lives inside me, and I've been afraid to own her.*
>
> *A terrorist lives inside me, and she'll quickly take you out.*
> *She loves to cry and stomp and lie, to whine, defy and pout.*
> *A terrorist lives inside me, and martyrdom is her game.*
> *She'll pour on you a ton of guilt, she'll make you wrong and blame.* ©2004

That silent, boiling anger is, in some ways, more lethal than physically expressed anger. It slowly and quietly kills off your relationships, your aliveness, your effectiveness, and your joy. Eventually, it may take out your health!

ANGER

Silently taking your unresolved anger out on people who love you isn't sexy. Turning anger silently inward isn't sexy, either. It makes you bitter, hard, and old before your time.

Have you taken a good, hard look at your anger? If you say you never get angry, I have to wonder whether you are dead. Because unlike what many of us have been taught, anger is normal and healthy.

You can learn to express your anger in positive ways once you get clear about what's at the bottom of it. Underneath much unexpressed anger is a whole bunch of pain.

Giving your pain a voice can turn your anger into healing energy for yourself and for others. Many Sexy Second Acts get started when people turn their pain into healthy anger.

Healthy anger, expressed and directed appropriately, can turn you into a game changer. Game changers are powerful and bodaciously badass sexy.

Think about game changers like Gandhi, Rosa Parks, and Martin Luther King, Jr.:

- I doubt Gandhi was in a dancing mood when he invited the British to leave India.
- Rosa Parks wasn't laughing much when she took that seat on the bus.
- Partying like a rock star wasn't high on Martin Luther King, Jr.'s agenda when he marched on Selma.

Gandhi, Martin Luther King, Jr., and Rosa Parks didn't set out to start movements. They just got good and mad. They were fed up and they decided to use their anger to make a difference.

They channeled their "madness." They drew a line in the sand. They stood up and spoke their truth in the face of daunting odds. They used their anger, rather than allowing their anger to use them.

Their anger became building blocks to futures that were never going to happen otherwise. Today we would call them "disrupters."

Disrupters are heroes. We recognize and honor them because that kind of heroism lives inside of each of us. If it didn't, we wouldn't see it in them. Doing something constructive with your anger makes you a hero in your own eyes, even if you never start a movement.

So how do you know if your anger is healthy? It's healthy when … :

- You see it as a signal that something is missing or not working.
- You know it's time to make a change for the better.
- It speaks your truth and is used for healing, not hurting.
- You aren't worried or concerned about survival because you are focused on a bigger vision.
- It isn't about winning for the sake of winning; it's about winning for a higher purpose.
- It comes from love, rather than hate.

Use the fire of your anger to burn unworkable stuff out of your life to make room for new growth. Burning old stuff works to renew forests; it works to renew your soul, too.

Allow your anger to just be. Learn to love, honor, and appreciate it. In the last verse of my poem, I began to speculate about how I could change my relationship with anger:

> *A terrorist lives inside me, but what if I could free her*
> *And allow myself to understand just what it's like to be her?*
> *Hello Terrorist, come out, come out, do not be afraid*
> *We'll work it out, we'll scream and shout; I think it's time we played.* ©2004

Get angry. Don't hide or suppress it. Use it to make a positive difference. There's a blessing in your anger if you hunt for it. The seeds of your purpose may dwell inside what angers you.

Purposeful anger, used wisely, is powerful, and bodaciously badass sexy.

ATTITUDE

It's no accident that "Attitude" starts with the first letter of the alphabet. Before you can change anything, you have to change your attitude.

How do you know whether your attitude is getting in your way or supporting you? Ask yourself how happy you are, how fulfilled you are, and how much joy you experience day-to-day.

Genuine, authentic attitude isn't about seeing yourself as better than anyone else, or being hurtful or mean. Genuine, authentic attitude is about confidence; accepting yourself exactly as you are; accepting life exactly as it is; and accepting others exactly as they are.

People with attitude don't worry about the opinions of others. They don't worry about being liked.

People with attitude either make the rules or break the rules. They don't worry about rules when breaking them serves a higher purpose.

People with attitude stand up for something even when there might be a high cost for doing it. Think about Paul Newman in *Cool Hand Luke*. Think about the young man who stood before the tank in Tiananmen Square. Think about *The Karate Kid*.

People with attitude are intelligent. They are up to something that matters.

Anger, combined with attitude, changes lives. I call it "badass-itude." Develop a healthy relationship with "badass-itude" and use it to change your world and contribute to changing the world around you.

Cultivate the attitude that you're the one and change begins with you. Don't throw your weight around. Stand up and be an example of the difference you want to make. Great leaders have attitude. Attitude is sexy!

AWARENESS

What a beautiful and powerful word. The practice of awareness can be one of the most rewarding and uplifting experiences available to you.

Most of the time we run on automatic pilot. We don't remember how we got to work, but there we are. We don't remember brushing our teeth or making the bed, but they got done. The television is turned on, but we don't remember what we watched five minutes after the program ends. We exist in a coma.

My friend Teri likens running on autopilot to having our eyeballs turned backward, looking into the past. We are looking into our heads, listening to "the committee" blather on about everything that's wrong with us, wrong with everyone else, and wrong with the world. Where's the sexy in that?

We don't look forward out of our eyes. We don't see the miracle of life as it unfolds around us, moment by moment. Being aware requires us to turn our eyeballs forward to look out at the world with delight, curiosity, wonder, and presence.

Rather than cultivating awareness, we are often rudely shocked into it. And it's generally not pretty.

A business associate shared a story of her own rude awakening into awareness. While she and her husband were driving on vacation, she fell asleep in the passenger seat. While she was napping, her husband fell asleep behind the wheel.

She was abruptly jolted awake by the ka-thump of their car hitting something. She didn't comprehend what had happened until someone explained it to her after it was all over. Their car had veered from the left-hand lane all the way across the highway to the right-hand lane, where they sideswiped a semi.

They were lucky. No other cars hit them. No one was hurt. They weren't dragged underneath the semi. They walked away from the accident with a few bruises on their bodies, minor scrapes on their vehicle, and a few extra gray hairs.

Talk about a wake-up call! Since then, she says she appreciates waking up every day. She is grateful for birds singing, her home, and her life. She is present to how beautiful everything is.

That's Awareness. Awareness is sexy! When you are aware and awake like that, life itself turns you on. You don't need anything else!

Money won't do it. "Stuff" won't do it. There's nothing that life has to give you. You know without a doubt that if you have life, you already have it all. Anything else you get is icing on the cake.

You can cultivate awareness in many ways. Meditation. Journaling. Walks in nature.

Spend time with a baby or a young child. They come into the world as full-out expressions of Divine Love. They haven't yet been messed up by language. There is no "committee" shouting at them inside their heads from morning till night.

Everything they see, touch, hear, taste, or smell is new and wonderful and exciting. You can see it in their bright and curious expressions.

Then go hang out with a teen. Notice the difference? Being cool overshadows delight, curiosity, and play.

Babies don't see flaws. By the time they reach their teens, they see flaws everywhere. In themselves, their friends, and their parents. Their love affair with life is replaced by boredom.

Until they fall in love. Love makes everything brand new again and brings you back to awareness. Love reminds you to look forward into the world, not backward into your head where the past lives.

When you fall in love, everything looks bright and new and shiny again. Love re-awakens all your senses. People in love are sexy.

You don't necessarily need to fall in love with another person. Fall in love with yourself. Have a love affair with your life. When you bring the juice back to your own life, you'll attract juicy partners to share it with.

They say to do at least one thing that scares you every day. Yes, that will wake you up, but I'm not convinced terror is a good motivator. Do something that enlivens you every day. The same chemicals are released, but your experience of the activity you chose will be different.

As you practice awareness, you may notice that time slows down and you become more peaceful and at ease in your own skin. How sexy would that feel?

"A" Remodeling Techniques:

- Pick an "A" word from this chapter as your theme for the day or week. Write it down and keep it with you.

- What resonates with you about this word? Journal your thoughts or meditate on them.

- Use your "A" word in conversation. Share what it means to you with someone. Ask that person to share what it means to him or her. Write down any insights that open up.

- Take at least one action consistent with the word you chose.

- Does a different "A" word resonate with you? Write it down and do the exercises on this page with the word you chose.

- Introduce awareness practices into your day. Do everything with your opposite hand. Drive a new route to work. Practice gratitude. Notice the wonder of how your body moves. Notice how you drive your car, type on your computer, or hug your kids. How do these practices alter your experience each day? Jot down any insights you have.

B

BADASS / BADASSITUDE / BADASSMANSHIP

Ever since I can remember, I've wanted to be a bona fide badass. It started in first grade when I was bullied on the playground at school.

Of course, I wouldn't have used that language when I was five. I just wanted to be big and tough enough to make the bullies leave me alone.

I've learned some things about badassery since first grade.

Being a bona fide badass isn't about breaking the law, scaring the socks off people, bullying them, or causing mayhem and destruction. It's about being true to yourself and living for what you believe in. Bona fide badasses don't want to hurt others—quite the opposite. They want to inspire, heal, and contribute.

It takes courage, integrity, and hard work to become an honest-to-goodness, bona fide badass. Like Louis Zamperini in the 2015 movie *Unbroken*, bona fide badasses have gone through hell and come out the other side with their integrity intact.

They don't go through hell because they want to. They do it because they have to, and they do it for the sake of something bigger than themselves.

Badasses don't worry about being proper or politically correct. They don't fit into a box, and that's why we love them. Bona fide badasses aren't even aware there is a box.

They work hard and play hard at what they love. Their eyes stay focused on the horizon as they gaze into the future, wondering what delightful, exciting, and fun game they can play or invent next.

My friend Laura is the Queen of bona fide badassmanship. And I mean that in the most complimentary way. She's one of my heroes. She's a mom, she's a business owner, and she's a philanthropist.

Nothing has been given to her. She's worked her butt off since she was a kid to earn every bit of everything she has.

You can always tell when Laura is up to something badass cool. You can see it coming. She gets a certain glint in her eye.

You never know what it's going to be. You just know you want to be in the vicinity, or in on the action when it shows up. You know it's gonna be out-of-the-box, badass fun.

I've learned a lot about bona fide badassmanship from Laura. I love this story she tells in a book by Claudia Cooley called *Savvy Women Revving Up for Success: Women Making a Difference in the World Today* (Claudia Cooley, Incorporated, 2015, pp. 64-67).

She started a brand new business. Within a few months, circumstances conspired against her and Laura didn't have enough money to make payroll. She tried everything she knew to raise the money, to no avail.

With nothing to lose, Laura took the last of the money from her business account and drove to Las Vegas on a Friday afternoon. She was determined to come back with the money she needed to make Monday's payroll.

That's badassmanship! She didn't give up. She kept looking for solutions, no matter how outrageously out of the box they were, until time ran out.

It would make a great story to say that she hit a huge jackpot in Vegas. That would be the stuff movies are made of. But no, she didn't come home with the whole amount. She did, however, come back with more money than she went there with.

And because she didn't give up, a solution for meeting her payroll showed up on Monday afternoon. I believe that's because the Universe saw Laura's commitment and sent that sassy vixen called Serendipity to give her an assist when she most needed it.

The money isn't the important part of this story. What makes Laura a bona fide badass is her willingness to put her butt on the line and not give up even in what appeared to be her darkest hour.

Maybe it takes a few hard knocks or maybe it requires you to get mad as hell and decide you're not going to take it anymore before you really get in touch with your inner bona fide badass. You have one inside you, whether or not you believe it.

If you want to be a bona fide badass, don't do it for notoriety. That's "thuggery." Being a badass without heart is being a bully.

Be a badass who makes something better for you, your relationship, your family, workplace, or community. That's sexy!

BODACIOUS

Certain words just roll deliciously off your tongue. Bodacious is one of those words.

Bodacious ups the ante on any word that follows it. Bodaciously badass. Bodacious acts of courage. Bodaciously talented.

You know it when you hear about someone who has done something bodacious. It leaves you smiling, and a little bit awed and inspired by whatever it was they did.

I'm not a big fan of anything that uses animals for the entertainment of humans. But I do kind of like this story about a Burma bull named Bodacious.

He was famous for a particular move where he put his head down and brought his hindquarters up. That forced the rider to lean forward. Bodacious would then bring his head up to smash the rider's face.

Bodacious's bodacious move caused so many serious injuries to riders, he had to be retired from the rodeo. As of this writing, you can see Bodacious in action on YouTube.

Bodacious was inducted into the ProRodeo Hall of Fame. I like to think he had a "Sexy Second Act" after leaving the rodeo. I picture him strutting around the pasture, telling tall tales to his offspring, and basking in his fame as the badassiest bull on the rodeo circuit.

There's a song called the "Ballad of Bodacious" by Les Claypool, Reid L. Lalonde III, and Bryan Kei Mantia. My favorite line is "Look out for Bodacious, he's bound to hold his ground."

If you're gonna be a bona fide badass, be a bodacious one. Hold your ground. Shake off anyone who tries to hold you back. You've got big dreams to accomplish.

People might not like you. But they are sure as heck going to respect you. Who knows? You might just end up in someone's Badass Hall of Fame someday. Wouldn't that be sexy?

BULLSHIT

I find that certain "shock" words add value to a conversation when they are used appropriately and selectively. "Nice" words just don't carry the same oomph.

When you let yourself relax and play with the idea that we are full of it at times, the word bullshit starts to lose its negative power. It can be used as a positive force for awareness.

No one I know of likes being called on their bullshit. I surely don't. It's often painful or embarrassing. It makes you look at stuff you'd rather avoid seeing. But there is nothing better than having a compassionate friend, colleague, or coach—who has your best interest at heart—yell "bullshit" when you need to hear it.

Bullshit is when you tell yourself stories about why you can't have the sexy, juicy, fun-tastic life and career you really want, even though you have no evidence that's the case. Bullshit is when you constantly talk about yourself negatively, thereby keeping yourself "stuck." It goes like this:

- I'm too old to change careers … bullshit!
- I'm not smart enough to be an entrepreneur … bullshit!
- I can't make a living doing what I really love … bullshit!

A former client came to me saying he wanted out of the career he was in. He felt like he didn't fit in with the company culture, and thought the excessive hours were taking a toll on his health.

For a time, he half-heartedly looked for a different situation. But he didn't stick with any of the ideas he came up with long enough to bring anything to fruition. There was always a reason it wasn't going to work.

This spilled over into his personal life, too. How you operate in one area of your life is often how you operate everywhere. He wanted many things to change, but if he took any action at all, he would come up against what he felt was a good reason not to move forward.

Finally, it was time to declare "bullshit" and acknowledge that he wasn't ready to step out of his comfort zone. And that's perfectly OK.

Acknowledging you aren't ready beats the heck out of wasting time and energy pretending. I believe he wants a better situation; he just doesn't want it badly enough (yet) to put his butt on the line to make the changes he needs to make.

Calling "bullshit" on yourself, like my client did, is courageous. The committee in his head may have a strong grip on him now, but by not resisting it, he may trick himself into a breakthrough one day. When that happens, I believe he will design an awesome Sexy Second Act!

If you are ready to design your Sexy Second Act, start by questioning what you think and believe. Just because it hasn't been done (yet) or you haven't done it (yet), there is no reason to think it can't be done.

Where are you holding yourself back from creating your bodaciously badass Sexy Second Act? Calling "bullshit" on your thinking is a way to hit the pause button on the naysaying committee in your head long enough to listen carefully to your heart.

Science is learning that our hearts are surrounded by a magnetic field that is 5000 times stronger than the magnetic field surrounding our brains. Yet we let our heads run the show. To me, that's like allowing Hal, the computer from the movie *2001: A Space Odyssey* take over the space ship. Mayhem ensues!

Put your attention on your heart. Listen for its clear, still voice. Every time the committee takes over and wants to steer you back to what's "practical" or to the "rational" mundane existence you've been living, holler "bullshit!"

Give yourself permission to stay true to your visions, dreams, and goals. Stick with it, stay curious, and your heart will give you an answer. That's sexy!

BUZZWORD

I doubt many people would include "buzzword" in their sexy building block list. When put in a different context than the one you may be familiar with, it can be a bodaciously badass word.

What words make you "buzz" and vibrate right down to your toes with delight? Sure, there are the obvious ones—like sex, orgasm, hot abs, and that wonderful old standby—chocolate!

But, let's stretch your imagination beyond the obvious. What words or phrases ignite a fire inside you?

"Shift happens" immediately when a business associate of mine talks about old cars. Whether he's talking about restoring them, driving them, or looking at pictures of them, he goes from looking tired and stressed to sparkling like a little kid. His excitement is infectious.

He's "buzzed." His entire body comes alive and vibrates with vitality and total fun.

Therein lies possible seeds for creating his Sexy Second Act. It will be fun to see what grows out of watering and nurturing those seeds. He's almost ready to begin. For now, he's still trying to figure it all out. I look forward to the day when he stops thinking so much and lets his "sexy" out to play.

"Old cars" isn't everyone's buzzword phrase. But when my associate gets buzzed talking about them, you can't help but get buzzed about them, too. You want to support and encourage his dream.

A friend's buzzword is "baseball." One summer, he drove across the country, visiting as many baseball games and stadiums as he could.

He had a blast. Baseball is his passion. Visiting every major stadium was his purpose. Having a wonderful time was his "paycheck."

What are your buzzwords? Make a list. Talk about them. Make a game of figuring out how to include as many "buzz-filled" activities and experiences as you can possibly fit into one lifetime.

You'll be delighted with the shift in your energy when you think about and talk about only what buzzes you. You'll powerfully be able to shift other people's energy, and they'll start talking about what buzzes them.

That's when the fun begins. Start supporting each other to design, build, and share buzz-filled activities and experiences. Watch how quickly everybody turns sexy!

"B" Remodeling Techniques:

- Pick your favorite "B" word from this chapter as your theme for the day or week. Write it down and keep it with you.

- Use your "B" word in conversation. Share with someone what it means to you. Ask what it means to him or her. Write down any insights that open up.

- Take at least one action consistent with the word you chose.

- Does a different "B" word resonate with you? Write it down and do the exercises on this page with the word you chose.

- Who are your "Bodaciously Badass" role models? Make a list of at least three. Is there a theme or pattern to the qualities you admire? Write them down. How can you include those qualities as you design and build your Sexy Second Act?

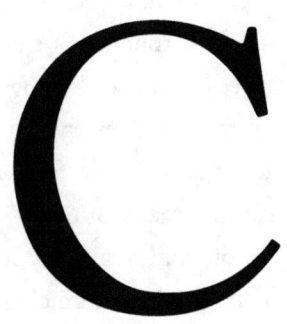

CHAMPION

The Olympics are amazing, both for the sports and for the touching human stories of athletes who participate. Learning how they climbed to this apex in their lives is fascinating.

Many have overcome seemingly insurmountable obstacles on their way to the Olympics. That makes them champions in my book, whether or not they go on to win medals.

What pulls them forward despite sometimes overwhelming odds? A compelling vision.

Is it the vision of winning a medal? I doubt it. What's a medal worth in terms of dollars and cents? Not much. It's the vision of what the medal represents that makes it priceless to those striving to win one.

Vision pulls champions out of bed every day to train, train, and train some more. Vision keeps them going in the face of defeat and daunting life circumstances that would crumple many of us.

Champions don't worry about failures. They lose many times. They fall. They sometimes lose heart. What makes them champions is their willingness to get back in the game every time they fall, fail, or lose.

Championship is about going for your vision and giving it your best shot. Going for it—no matter how it turns out—will keep you from going to the grave with regrets.

What's your Olympic medal? What's your championship game? You can be a champion whether you want to start a business, climb Mount Everest, or graduate from college.

You just have to make your vision compelling enough to pull you out of bed every day in the face of any obstacle. You have to create a bodaciously badass vision that's bigger than your fear. You might not stand on a podium in front of millions to receive a medal for the championship game you create. But, when you get in it, beat the odds and win it, how sexy will it be to hear the *Rocky* theme song playing in your head as you raise your fists into the air in a victory salute?

CHAOS

My friend Laura leads what often seems like a chaotic life. She has so many plates spinning, I'm amazed they don't all come crashing down.

Once, when I was in a particularly scattered state, I asked her how she kept them all spinning. She laughed. "Chaos is good!" she exclaimed.

That's become one of my mantras.

The truth is that she occasionally does drop a plate or two. But what I've noticed is that when she drops one, it's deliberate. She knows who she is and what she's up to, so she lets go of "shiny object" plates quickly. She stays focused on spinning only those plates that align with her vision and mission. Having a vision and mission are great tools to have in your toolbox for staying focused when chaos threatens to take you off course.

This book project started from chaos when my Mastermind Group challenged me to write a book in thirty days. My first thought was, "No way!" The committee in my head chimed in to tell me it was impossible and overwhelming. But my heart knew it was time for me to do it.

When you allow yourself to surrender and genuinely entertain an idea that comes from your heart, Serendipity comes out to play. Solutions and assistance show up in fascinating and wonderful ways.

Shortly after accepting the challenge, I stumbled upon my inspirational word plaque in a gift shop. I read about a website that challenges you to write a minimum of 750 words per day. It helped that the website provides reminders and incentives to keep you on track to write every day.

A lot can happen in thirty days. Thirty days of writing at least 750 words a day was enough to get me close to the total number of words I needed to fill a book.

Thirty days of free-writing shifted my perception. Something I thought was impossible—writing a book—now seemed doable.

Thirty days taught me to appreciate that chaos is part of the creative process. "Shitty first draft" is just another term for chaos!

Thirty days of giving myself permission to create freely brought some seemingly unconnected things together:

- my desire to write a book
- a challenge tossed out by my Mastermind Group
- a plaque I bought on a whim
- a theme for the book.

Out of chaos comes order. When you act on your creative ideas, dots connect. Order emerges.

In the midst of chaos, when it appears nothing substantial exists, everything is possible. Keep that in mind, especially when you experience a blowup or a mess-up—like a divorce or job loss.

From a state of chaos, you have an infinite ability to delve into what is important to you. Give yourself permission to create "shitty first drafts," whether it's finding your way as a single person, looking for a sexy new job, learning to paint, writing a book or a blog post, trying out a business idea, buying your first house, or learning to skateboard.

Embrace the chaos. Use it to create something "sexy" that matters to you. In the process, you will discover more of who you truly are. There's nothing sexier than that!

CHOCOLATE

Chocolate is happy food. No matter how bad a situation is, chocolate makes it better. Say the word and it puts a smile on almost everyone's face. The word "chocolate" represents giving yourself permission to indulge in, and enjoy, the sweet things in life.

Years ago, my friend Teri and I conjured up a sweet celebration ritual that's always fun. It started when we led seminars together. One time, during a meal break, we ordered bread pudding and whiskey sauce for dessert to celebrate a successful and transformational day.

When our waiter brought our check, he asked us how our meal was. We teased him by saying the bread pudding was great, but the whiskey sauce was a bit light on whiskey.

We were kidding. It was perfect.

We returned to the same restaurant the next time we led a seminar. We were served by the same waiter, and we again ordered the bread pudding and whiskey sauce for dessert. Our waiter caught us completely by surprise when he delivered our dessert with an impish smile and an extra shot of whiskey on the side.

We laughed and laughed. The bread pudding tasted doubly delicious. The waiter got a lovely tip. We all had a great time. We left the restaurant that day feeling a bit tipsy and with a warm glow in our hearts.

Bread pudding and whiskey sauce became our sweet celebration reward. We now order it for all sorts of celebrations ... birthdays, holidays, sometimes even Tuesdays. We make up reasons to celebrate.

Chocolate, or bread pudding and whiskey sauce, represents life's sweet delights. Dessert. Laughter. Friendship. Playful service from a caring waiter who does that extra something to bring a smile to his customers' faces.

What makes life sweet for you? Give yourself permission to enjoy it, unabashedly. No excuses. No apologies. No guilt. Just feel the sexy!

COMMITMENT

Commitment is a radical word. People have a love/hate relationship with it. We commit without giving much thought to what commitment truly means. We habitually "overcommit" and then fall short on following through. This includes when:

- We commit to marriage and then we cheat.
- We commit to doing a job and we wind up doing shoddy work.
- We purchase something on credit and then renege on paying the bill on time.

The cost of dishonoring our commitments is high—physically, spiritually, emotionally, and financially.

Two life experiences taught me the value of commitment. The first was going back to college to complete my degree. The second was skydiving.

I knew that going back to school to get my Bachelor's Degree while working was not going to be easy, but I'd wanted to do it for years. I got tired of thinking about it. I got tired of hearing about how not having it was holding me back in my career. I finally decided to bite the bullet and get it done.

One night, just a few months short of graduation, I was working late to finish part of my senior project to meet a deadline. Wouldn't you know it, something happened with my computer and I lost my entire seventy-five page document.

I couldn't believe it! I had no backup copy. I would have to start over. I was devastated. I "hit the wall." I couldn't graduate without completing the project. I honestly didn't know if I had it in me to keep going. I wasn't even sure I wanted to.

The committee in my head immediately jumped in and started yammering: "Getting a degree is too hard." "You should just give up for being such a dummy and messing up so badly." "You can't do anything right, so why bother?"

It would have been easy to walk away. But I remembered my vision. I saw

COMMITMENT

myself walking across the stage to get my diploma. I felt how proud my family would be of me. I pictured my diploma hanging on my wall and how it would feel to finally be able to say, "Yes! I'm a college grad!"

My heart knew that if I walked away from that vision, I would always regret it. I picked myself up off the floor, where I'd collapsed into a puddle of tears, and got back to work.

Later that year, my dream came true. I completed my degree program and graduated. My family was in attendance, cheering my accomplishment. The day turned out even better than I imagined.

That was my Olympic moment. My diploma was my gold medal.

Commitment is about wanting something badly enough to do whatever it takes to succeed. When necessary, you must be willing to pull yourself through the eye of the needle to accomplish your dream.

Here's a "litmus test" you can use for evaluating whether or not to commit to something. Question how you are going to feel if you don't do it.

Will you be disappointed? If you quit, will you be left wondering, "What if?"

Skydiving taught me some unforgettable lessons about commitment. It started with that breathtaking moment when we leaped out of the airplane, and I realized there was nothing but air between me and the ground.

The jump happened so fast, my brain was on total overload. I couldn't properly process the experience. My brain was shouting, "Oh, crap! What the hell did you just do?" If you want to know what it's like to be 100% in Act II and looking forward out of your eyes, go skydiving!

It was only later, after hours of watching and re-watching the video, that I absorbed a few things about commitment:

- Before committing, decide what outcome you want. Create an inspiring intention that reflects that outcome. My intention was to conquer fear.
- Commit as though your life depends on it. Jump in as if there is no going back. If you can't jump in like that, maybe this isn't something you truly want.

- Get the help of experts who have been there. I jumped with an expert skydiver who had over a thousand jumps to his credit.
- Have faith. My friend Karen says, "Sometimes you just have to jump and let the wind take you." Once you jump, there's nothing to do but ride the experience. Faith requires you to let go and leave the rest to God.
- Find accountability partners. I may never have gone skydiving if I hadn't gone with a group of friends, all of whom were holding each other accountable for following through.

Choose carefully what you commit to. If your answer to how you'll feel if you don't do it is that you'll feel relieved, don't do it! That can be a brave choice to make.

If you treat what you commit to as being so important that your life depends on it, would you settle for a job you hate? Would you marry someone without knowing who he was or what he was committed to? Would you buy that house "hoping" you'd be able to pay the mortgage?

What are you willing to exchange the precious moments of your life for? Because, like it or not, you are limited to a certain number of years on the planet. Do you truly want to spend them committing to anything other than what matters most?

My guess is you aren't going to lie on your death bed celebrating your million-dollar mansion, hourglass figure, or your trophy spouse. You'll want to remember your Olympic medal and bread-pudding-and-whiskey-sauce moments that you spent with colleagues, friends, and family.

Do a little soul-searching. Are you committing to things that don't really matter or that cause you grief and pain? Make a plan to give them up. Create sexy new commitments worthy of your precious time, energy, and talents. Go in the direction of bodaciously badass joy!

COMMUNITY

The dictionary describes community as an assembly of people who live in the same area, or who share the same interests. By that definition, it doesn't matter if they know or care about each other. For example, how many people do you know in your neighborhood, professional association, or church community?

But what if there was a different kind of community? What if you belonged to a community with whom you created an agreement to exchange nothing but love, trust, acceptance, and support?

If you are lucky, you have that level of community in your family, but it doesn't always work that way. In that case, you may have to design and build your community. It could be a Mastermind Group, your book club, or your golf buddies.

Effective communities are safe places to open up. They allow you to relax to a point where you can be vulnerable and share your innermost desires and fears. They create a place where you catch each other when you fall, support each other to get back on your feet, and celebrate each other's victories.

In trusted communities, people listen without judgment. They support each other's dreams no matter how crazy-wild-off-the-charts weird they are. At the same time, they are willing to call you on your bullshit and tell you what you need to hear, not just what you want to hear.

People listen differently in a community where they are accepted exactly the way they are. Where people listen from their hearts. Where they hear the beauty of your unique song. Through them, you learn to hear your heart's song over the din of the committee in your head—maybe for the first time. Your personal truth is revealed in the acceptance and trust of a supportive community.

A few of my girlfriends got together and made an agreement that we would never say anything about each other that we wouldn't say to each other. No gossiping. The agreement is that if we slip up, we have to 'fess up to the person we talked about. We don't always agree with each other, but we always know where we stand with each other.

You are blessed if you have that kind of community. Not many people do.

No one can accomplish big things in life alone. If we could, we'd be clever enough to have done it by now. We need the support of others to help accomplish the things that matter most.

It may take time and patience to create, but do the work to find your community. It's worth the effort to give yourself the gift of a supportive community. You deserve it.

CONGRUENCE

We humans are incredibly designed—perhaps the best "machines" ever created. And yet, we generally take better care of our cars and pets than we take of ourselves.

You have a built-in "thermostat" that tells you whether your mind, heart, spirit and body are operating congruently. It's simple and accurate when you tune in long enough to take a measurement:

- Congruent – in the zone, happy, relaxed, effortlessly productive, feeling gratitude, contributing, fulfilled, expansive, loving, playful
- Incongruent – sad, angry, depressed, anxious, shut down, in pain, blaming, selfish.

A client demonstrated this distinction perfectly. She had several exciting goals, but she wasn't taking consistent action.

I start our weekly coaching call by asking how her week went. Her tone of voice quickly clues me in to how much progress she makes on her goals.

She sounds stressed and exhausted when she hasn't completed the actions she promised to undertake. She speaks in a low, slow monotone.

She means it when she commits to taking specific actions each week. But between calls, she gets in her own way. She procrastinates. Avoids. Makes excuses. The committee in her head outshouts her heart, telling her she's lazy, helpless, and incompetent.

The difference in her energy is quickly apparent when she follows through. You hear enthusiasm in her voice as she shares her results.

By pointing out the difference in her energy, she is recognizing her pattern. Not taking action between sessions is congruent with the way she thinks about herself as lazy, slow, and incompetent.

That thought pattern is incongruent with the bright, funny, talented and capable woman she truly is. Her low energy is the signal from her body telling her she isn't aligning her actions with what her heart truly wants.

She is learning to stop beating herself up when she goes off course. She is learning to pay attention to her "energy temperature" so she can interrupt the pattern of her old, limited thinking. She is replacing her old beliefs with new ones that are consistent with who she is and what she wants.

She is now well on her way to creating a fabulous future that energizes her. She's giving herself permission to enjoy the journey. Step-by-step she's finding course-correcting to be quicker, easier, and more fun. She's excited about the results she's getting, which is the momentum she needs to keep herself moving happily forward.

Become your own thermostat. Take your "energy temperature" several times a day. Notice how energized, awake, and alive you feel. If your energy is down, see if you can identify patterns of thinking that drain your energy.

Recalibrate your thermostat by designing empowering beliefs that bring you into alignment with joy, appreciation and gratitude. Make adjustments that raise your energy temperature to the point where you hum with vitality, excitement, and sexy-hot passion!

"C" Remodeling Techniques:

- Pick your favorite "C" word from this chapter as your theme for the day or week. Write it down and keep it with you.

- Use your "C" word in conversation. Share with someone what it means to you. Ask what it means to him or her. Write down any insights that open up.

- Take at least one action consistent with the word you chose.

- Does a "C" word not on this list resonate with you? Write it down and do the exercises on this page with the word you chose.

- Make a list of the people in your life who you believe truly have your back and would agree to set up regularly scheduled meetings or phone calls to share and support each other's dreams and goals. Keep track of the results.

- Take your joy temperature on a scale of one to ten. If it's a seven or above most of the time, create your "bread pudding and whiskey sauce" reward! You're on a roll! If it's lower than a seven most of the time, look for areas of incongruence. What adjustments would it take to get you vibrating at an eight, nine, or ten in that area?

D

DANCE

It surprises me when I run into someone who doesn't like to dance. How is it possible for people to go through life without craving to move their bodies to music? Next to sex, dancing is the easiest and most enjoyable way to bring yourself into the present moment. Okay, okay, maybe sports and exercise do the same thing for some people.

The point is that, like sex, dancing is a form of surrender. It's a form of vulnerability. But where sex is generally done in private, dancing is generally done in public. Perhaps dance haters experience performance anxiety in public, so it's easier to just say no.

That's too bad. Dancing isn't about getting the steps right. That certainly has its place if you love competitive dancing. But for most of us, dancing is a sensual form of play.

Dancing by yourself gives you an opportunity to express yourself. Dancing with a partner gives you an opportunity to make an intimate connection. Dancing in a community, such as when you line dance, gives you the opportunity to share a common experience.

Resisting the music, or your dance partner, ruins the flow and breaks the rhythm. Connecting becomes impossible. How can you resist and connect at the same time?

Life works the same way. Fighting it ruins the flow and makes it really hard. Overthinking the steps is likely to trip you up.

But what a difference when you relax and surrender to rhythm of the dance! It may feel awkward in the beginning, but as you practice, it begins to flow. You start to experience life's beauty, elegance, and joy! It seems effortless. And you might find yourself living as William Purkey suggests:

"You've gotta dance like there's nobody watching,
Love like you'll never be hurt,
Sing like there's nobody listening,
And live like it's heaven on earth."

DANCE

What if you believed that life was your dance partner and not something to be survived or dominated? What if life gets a giggle out of your sassy, badass, flirty self and can't wait to dance with you? Foxtrot, polka, or even the occasional twerk. How would that make a difference in the choices you make?

DECLARATION

Declarations move energy from your inner world to the outer world of manifestation. They come from the desires of your heart. When you want to make something happen, declare it! Just like:

- "I will graduate from college."
- "I will survive."
- "As God is my witness, I'll never be hungry again." (Scarlett O'Hara in Gone With the Wind)
- "I will escape from (the barrio, the ghetto, my addiction, abuse)."
- "I may not get there with you, but ... I want you to know ... that as a people, we will get to the Promised Land." (Martin Luther King, Jr.)

Declarations are powerful because they come from your inner certainty that you are going to give it all you've got and more. Nothing is going to stop you until you achieve your goal. That energy is called willpower.

When our forefathers decided it was time to break away from Britain, they didn't write the Manifesto of Independence or Thoughts about Independence or the Wish for Independence. They wrote the *Declaration of Independence.*

They literally put skin in the game, knowing what might happen. There was no certainty it would work out. Our forefathers put their lives and fortunes on the line for American independence, and many of them paid a high price. But despite the odds against them, independence was won. The power of that declaration still resonates with us today.

Motivational speaker T. Harv Eker understands the power of declarations. He often asks participants to place their hands over their hearts and make a declaration out loud. I spoke one that led to a huge breakthrough in identifying a limiting belief I held about money, opening the door to transforming it.

The declaration was, "My parents' beliefs about money are not me and not mine." When I said it out loud with my hand over my heart, I began to cry. That surprised me.

DECLARATION

It took a few days of journaling and digging inside to figure out where the tears came from. It seemed like my dad was always looking over my shoulder when it came to finances. Even after I grew up and lived on my own, he questioned my every major purchase to make sure I could handle it and that I was not using up all my savings.

I knew he was concerned and wanted to make sure I took good financial care of myself. But inside, I felt like he didn't trust me to do so. No matter how much I demonstrated that I was financially responsible, he never said, "I'm proud of you," or "Good job!"

That declaration surfaced how much it hurt me that my dad never acknowledged me for being a good money manager. I saw how I kept trying to "prove" it, not only to him, but to myself.

Was it true that my dad wasn't proud of me? I'm sure he was. By this time, I couldn't ask him, because he'd already passed on.

What I could do was let go of trying to prove something to him—and myself—that was unprovable. I could let go of the hurt and be proud of myself for my ability to be financially responsible. I could feel gratitude toward my dad for teaching me good money habits. I could make a new declaration that gave me power. And that is exactly what I did:

"I easily attract money in fun, creative, and exciting ways that meet my needs and bring me satisfaction, joy, and peace of mind."

Declarations aren't real until you get them out of your head. Write them down. Say them to yourself out loud. Put extra skin in the game by declaring your dreams out loud to trusted friends or associates who support you and will hold you accountable for following through.

It takes courage to make a declaration. They are powerful. Negative declarations like, "I'll never amount to anything," are just as powerful. So be careful what you declare.

By making a declaration, you are putting your word into the future as a promise and a commitment. Promise yourself to make only those declarations that honor your truth. They are valuable power tools to put in your toolbox to help you design and build your Sexy Second Act.

DESIRE

One of the most challenging tasks my clients face is distinguishing what they truly desire from what they think they should desire. It's no wonder, with all the interfering static we get from our culture and the media.

This isn't just a conversation for women, although women often carry around a few extra pieces of baggage—like how it's our responsibility to make sure everyone else's desires are taken care of first. Then maybe—just maybe—if the stars align just right and it's the "second Tuesday of the week," we get to take care of one or two of our own desires.

My training included completing a course specifically designed to help both men and women identify what they want. I thought I was the only one who didn't have a clue. I could not have been more wrong!

There are common themes:

- money
- to be happy and healthy
- to have happy and healthy relationships
- freedom and flexibility
- to make a difference .

The deer-in-headlights looks begin when you drill down to specifics:

- How much money?
- Exactly what makes you happy? What would it take for you to be healthy?
- How would you and your happy relationship partner and family spend time together? How would you know you were loved?
- What exactly would you like to do with your freedom and extra time?
- Exactly who would you like to make a difference for ... and how?

Deep inside, we know what we love. We know how to play. But we've been told we must be "adults" for so long, we think we have to give up what we love for the practical, and give up being playful for being responsible. As if they are incompatible. Who says we can't have it all? We just have to be willing to embrace the possibility.

The first answers people come up with are seldom "songs from the heart" responses. They are primarily ho-hum. Heart song answers shift your energy—and the energy of others—from boredom to playfulness and excitement.

Ho-hum: I'd like to travel.

Sexy: I want to sit on a hill in Tuscany, watching the sunset, with a glass of good wine in one hand and my camera in the other.

Ho-Hum: I'd like to start a business.

Sexy: I want to own a company where my clients enjoy their working relationship with me. I charge what I'm worth and I have money left over each month for savings. I have time in my schedule to serve my clients and also to work on creative projects I enjoy.

Ho-hum: I want to lose weight.

Sexy: I'm a healthy and fit old fart who remembers to go to sleep at a reasonable hour and wake up refreshed and ready to start the day. I eat healthy, exercise daily and keep a balanced schedule, spending quality time with friends and family outside the work environment.

Pay attention to your desires—the authentic ones lying dormant deep within your heart. Get them out and dust them off. Look for a theme. Play with how you can use your theme as a solid building block for remodeling your life and designing specific, measurable, sexy-hot goals for your Second Act life and career.

"D" Remodeling Techniques:

- Pick your favorite "D" word from this chapter as your theme for the day or week. Write it down and keep it with you.

- Use your "D" word in conversation. Share with someone what it means to you. Ask what it means to them. Write down any insights that open up.

- Take at least one action consistent with the word you chose.

- Does a "D" word that's not on this list resonate with you? Write it down and do the exercises on this page with the word you chose.

- Want to release yourself from the tyranny of something unworkable in your life? Make a declaration. Put something at stake for building a Sexy Second Act career or life that matters to you. Share with a buddy who will support you and hold you accountable.

- Make a list of at least 50 desires. Rank them as:
  * On Fire – You would be, do or have them right now if you had the time or money.
  * Simmering – You'd like to do them eventually, after you fulfill your "on fire" desires.
  * Cool – Sounds like a good idea, but you'd be OK if you never got to them.
- Take at least one action toward accomplishing one of your "on fire" desires.

E

EMBRACE

Hugs are awesome. I love 'em. I don't think we hug enough. You've likely seen the studies stating that hugs are good for your health. But dang it all, hugs just feel good! Do you need any other reason for hugging?

Then there's embracing. To embrace someone—or something—you must open your arms wide and expose your heart. You must allow yourself to become vulnerable.

If you find yourself fighting with someone, pause and try this experiment. Stand facing each other with your arms wide open as if you are about to embrace.

Stand close enough to touch. But without touching, embrace each other with your eyes, keeping your arms wide open. Look directly into each other's eyes without looking away. Keep your expression relaxed and speak only with your eyes. Do this for two minutes and then each share what it was like. Repeat as necessary.

Open your arms wide to embrace new and different ideas. Open your arms wide to embrace situations where you feel yourself closing off to someone whose beliefs or way of life are significantly different from yours.

See how long it takes for your anger and resistance to soften and for the heat to disappear from your words. See how long it takes for you to listen, rather than merely hear. See how long it takes before you have the desire to gather that person, or idea, into your heart and into your arms for a good, old-fashioned bodaciously badass bear hug!

ENLIGHTENMENT

In my opinion, "enlightened" people can be über annoying. They will drive you nuts. If you find someone who tells you they are enlightened, run! You can be pretty sure they don't truly get what it is.

Enlightened isn't something you are. Rather, it's an ongoing process of becoming. It's a path to travel, not a destination, result, or outcome. You are headed for trouble if you look to achieve enlightenment as a goal. In personal growth circles, I often hear it said that yesterday's transformation is today's ego trip.

Ego trips take you to a destination my friend Karen calls "True Believer Syndrome." Someone suffering from True Believer Syndrome makes himself an authority figure and puts himself above others. True Believers want to force others to come around to their way of thinking. Where's the sexy in that?

True Believer Syndrome is different from being true to your beliefs. When you are true to your beliefs, you live them. You share them without forcing them on anyone. You share with the intention to support and uplift. Sharing beliefs is an exploration that leads to the discovery of deeper and wider truths.

No two people have exactly the same point of view, because each of us has a unique experience of living. Enlightenment includes the notion that everyone's point of view is valid, whether or not you agree with it.

The question to ponder is how workable particular points of view are. If they lean toward compassion, joy and making life better, they are enlightened points of view. If they don't, they point to something that needs attention to make it workable. Enlightenment is the acceptance that all points of view are an opportunity to be curious, to listen, to learn, and to grow.

This poem by John Godfrey Saxe beautifully describes how things get distorted when we limit ourselves to a single point of view:

> *"It was six men of Indostan, to learning much inclined,*
> *who went to see the elephant (Though all of them were blind),*
> *that each by observation, might satisfy his mind.*

*"The first approached the elephant, and, happening to fall,
against his broad and sturdy side, at once began to bawl:
God bless me! but the elephant, is nothing but a wall!'*

*"The second feeling of the tusk, cried: 'Ho! what have we here,
so very round and smooth and sharp? To me 'tis mighty clear,
this wonder of an elephant, is very like a spear!'
The third approached the animal, and, happening to take,
the squirming trunk within his hands, 'I see,' quoth he,
the elephant is very like a snake!'*

*"The fourth reached out his eager hand, and felt about the knee:
'What most this wondrous beast is like, is mighty plain,' quoth he;
'Tis clear enough the elephant is very like a tree.'*

*"The fifth, who chanced to touch the ear, Said; 'E'en the blindest man
can tell what this resembles most; Deny the fact who can,
This marvel of an elephant, is very like a fan!'*

*"The sixth no sooner had begun, about the beast to grope,
than, seizing on the swinging tail, that fell within his scope,
'I see,' quoth he, 'the elephant is very like a rope!'*

*"And so these men of Indostan, disputed loud and long,
each in his own opinion, exceeding stiff and strong.
Though each was partly in the right, and all were in the wrong!*

*"So, oft in theologic wars, the disputants, I ween,
tread on in utter ignorance, of what each other mean,
and prate about the elephant, not one of them has seen!"*

ENLIGHTENMENT

Rather than fight for a single point of view, what if the six men of Indostan embraced, shared, and discussed each other's points of view? What if they accepted that each point was equally valid? Do you think they might have developed a more accurate, and enlightened, picture of the elephant?

Next time you find yourself in a disagreement, try looking at it from the other person's point of view before you rush to judgment. You may gain a perspective that hadn't occurred to you before.

How do you know you are on the path of enlightenment? You feel relaxed, open, joyful, accepting, and inclusive.

Walk that path and you will discover unlimited reserves of power, energy, and attraction within you. Now, that is totally sexy!

EPIPHANY

Epiphanies are delicious. I like to think of them as spiritual orgasms. There's a buildup of tension or excitement until you suddenly break through to a brand new and more expansive world of consciousness. Epiphanies are milestones of awareness that you experience on your path toward enlightenment.

They open the door to a fresh start. They give you a wider perception and greater appreciation for your life journey to this point. As you look toward the future, you see new and exciting possibilities that pull you happily into action.

Resistance is one indicator that you are on your way to an epiphany. We often treat resistance as our enemy, but it can also be our ally, pointing us to something within us that needs work or needs healing.

In his book, *Do the Work*, author Stephen Pressfield says that the more important the calling or action is to the evolution of your soul, the more resistance you will experience. That notion alone can lead you to an epiphany!

At the very least, it makes it easier to embrace the discomfort associated with resistance. If you experience resistance, throw your arms wide open to embrace it in anticipation that if you stay with it, you are headed toward an epiphany that will open you up to exciting possibilities.

Openness is key. If you run away from the discomfort of resistance, epiphanies won't chase after you. But resistance will. It will hunt you down like a dog and eat you alive.

Turn and face it. Don't gaze resistance in its eye. Look beyond it to the Sexy Second Act you want badly enough to stop resistance in its tracks. Keep moving in that direction toward an epiphany that will melt resistance away like an ice cube in the sun on a hot summer's day.

EXCELLENCE

Are you on a perfection hamster wheel? Why not jump off, relax, and trade perfection for living a life of excellence? Design excellent relationships, career, business, financial, health, and spiritual practices.

The day I finally gave up perfection was an excellent day. Giving it up occurred while I was listening to a program about the Enneagram, a study of human personality.

The speaker said that perfection is a bar you can never reach. He said that when you get to where you think perfection is, you discover that there is a higher level to reach for.

I had to listen to that again. I was having an epiphany.

I realized I had been playing a no-win game with perfection. It was a crazy-making game set up by others: the media, our culture, our gender, caregivers, and the generation we were born into.

The crazy-making and agonizing truth is all around us. The media, and advertising in particular, set the bar on "perfection" impossibly high. We torture ourselves emotionally and physically, and make ourselves nuts trying to measure up. We end up feeling like we can never win, so we give up and feel bad about ourselves.

No wonder depression abounds on an epic scale! Perfection is exhausting and self-sabotaging. We mutilate our bodies, minds, and spirits trying to achieve the impossible!

I realized it was time for me to jump off the perfection hamster wheel and simply allow myself to breathe. It was such a relief to let perfection go! I chose to trade it in for Excellence.

We call the highest rank in any Olympic event "a perfect 10." But it isn't really "perfect," is it? A "10" in the next Olympics will not be the same as a "10" was in the last Olympics.

Why? Because if a perfect "10" existed, the Olympic Games as we know them would become obsolete. Once you achieve perfection, there is nowhere else to go.

Can you imagine watching golf if legendary golfer Tiger Woods hit a hole-in-one on every single hole at every single tournament? You would eventually stop watching him. The fun would be gone if you already knew the outcome. Perfection equals "game over."

You'd switch to watching athletes coming up behind him to see who was going to be next. As more golfers achieved that level of perfection, golf course architects would have to redesign them to make them more challenging. Or the entire game of golf would require remodeling.

Perfection isn't what humans love. We love the pursuit of excellence.

We humans love challenges and we admire excellence. Excellence keeps the game in play. Perfection ends it. Games are fun. You can play for excellence again and again for as long as you enjoy the game.

If you are living your life in pursuit of perfection, let it go. Strive for excellence. What would your life look like if you were living it as an excellent adventure? What steps can you take now to begin moving in that direction?

"E" Remodeling Techniques:

- Pick your favorite "E" word from this chapter as your theme for the day or week. Write it down and keep it with you.

- Use your "E" word in conversation. Share with someone what it means to you. Ask what it means to him or her. Write down any insights that open up.

- Take at least one action consistent with the word you chose.

- Does an "E" word that's not on this list resonate with you? Write it down and do the exercises on this page with the word you chose.

- Think back over your life and see how many epiphanies you can identify. How did they change the direction of your life? What do you see or appreciate differently as a result?

- Pick an area of your life where you've been striving for perfection. If you let go of perfection and committed to excellence, how would your attitude change? How would you approach that area differently?

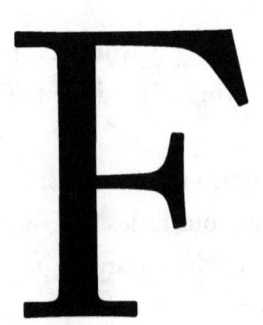

FAILURE

Failure might seem like a weird word to put into a book about powerful language. I included it because it's such a "hot button" for many of us.

It took me a long time to understand that there's a gift in failure that gives you power. To receive the gift, you must first distinguish the difference between failure as an event and being a failure.

Until I learned that distinction, fear of failing kept me from doing an uncountable number of things I wanted to do. I felt like a pretzel sometimes, spiritually and emotionally contorting myself into inwardly weird shapes to keep from failing.

Failing felt like humiliation in my world. Nothing felt worse.

The paradox was that by trying so hard not to fail, I felt like a failure anyway. What you resist, persists.

A coach helped me transform my relationship with failure. He assigned me the task of deliberately failing four times in a single week.

Omigod! That was painful! Not wanting to fail, I spent the entire week between calls agonizing over how to fail four times. How do you deliberately fail?

Maybe there's a way to deliberately fail, but I didn't figure it out. I failed my assignment to fail, and I went to my next coaching call ready to be chastised for failing to complete my assignment.

Rather than chastising me, my coach laughed. That didn't make me feel any better, until he helped me recognize that the point of the assignment was to have me look at what I made failure mean.

It was an epiphany to see how firm a grip the fear of failing had on me. Seeing it was the beginning of letting it go.

When you or I fail, the world won't stop spinning on its axis. The sun will still come up every day. The people who love us will still love us. What a concept!

Failure is an opportunity for you to see what you are made of. Are you willing to learn from your failure? Are you willing to pick yourself up and try again? And again? And, yet again?

The one thing worse than failure is regret. Risk is part of the deal. Skydiving taught me that.

Something can always go wrong. Going after my degree taught me that.

If it was all smooth sailing, how would we grow? Remind yourself of that by telling yourself you are experiencing "growing pains" when things don't work out.

When something comes along that I want to do, but I'm scared I won't be able to pull it off, I ask myself, "How am I going to feel if I don't do this?" And if there is the tiniest indication I will regret not doing it, I know I must give it a shot. Sometimes you just have to give faith a chance.

If you are afraid of failure, I dare you to stand in front of a mirror, look yourself smack-dab in the eye, square your shoulders, put your hands on your hips, and "declare" that fear is no longer allowed to stand between you and your dreams.

Give yourself a Tiger Woods victory fist pump and tell yourself you've got this! And then get out there and create something sexy and excellent.

FIERCE

When I think of fierceness, I think of mama bears. Or mamas, in general. Stand between a mama and her babies and you'll soon find out what fierce looks like. If you live long enough.

Fierceness is about protecting and defending things that matter. Children. The environment. Freedom. Ideas. Independence. Love. Dreams.

Being fierce means putting your butt on the line. Being fierce is being unstoppable.

The men who wrote and signed the Declaration of Independence were fierce. So was the young man who stood alone against the tanks in Tiananmen Square; Dr. King when he marched to Selma; and the passengers aboard Flight 93 on September 11th when they said those final, fateful words, "Let's Roll."

My friend Teri shared this definition of fierceness she learned from Business Coach Martin Sage of Sage University:

"Fierceness is an actualized state in the world of being awake and playing a life game of win-win as opposed to playing a fear-based game of win-lose or lose-lose. It's about taking responsibility and owning all of your life."

Components of living fiercely include:

- taking responsibility for your choices
- forgiving yourself for choices that didn't work out
- forgiving others who have caused you harm
- learning from your mistakes and applying what you've learned to design a life of better choices
- embracing the unknown with courage, commitment, curiosity, and play
- becoming so clear about who you are and what you want that you effortlessly set boundaries around your time, priorities, and energy

- surrounding yourself with like-minded people who support you and whom you support in return.

You have fierceness within you, whether you believe it or not. The world needs your ferocity and passion more than ever now.

What do you care about? What would you like to see change for the better?

There are a gazillion problems that need tackling. GMOs, starving children, global warming. You name it.

You have a choice. You can stand on the sidelines and complain. You can rant on social media. Or you can put on your fierce warrior gear, be willing to put your butt on the line, and take action about something that matters to you.

Either way, you are going to die someday. Do you want to be remembered as a hater or spectator? Or would you rather be remembered as a fierce doer and sexy difference-maker?

FOCUS

I grew up believing that discipline was either about punishment or hard work. Either way, it was distasteful to me. To this day, I prefer the word "focus."

I read somewhere that you must be willing to dive headlong into the depths of your obsessions. That's a pretty good way to look at focus. Diving headlong into the depths of your obsessions eliminates distraction and keeps everything clear and simple.

It's challenging to stay focused these days, with so many things demanding your attention. Here are some tools to include in your Focus Toolkit:

- Dive headlong into a big, juicy, exhilarating dream you are willing and eager to pursue.
- Determine why it matters.
- Choose a direction in the form of a goal. Like Yogi Berra said, "If you don't know where you are going, you might wind up someplace else."

Other focus tools include meditation; setting intentions; creating vision boards; hiring a coach; joining a mastermind group; and creating a mission or purpose statement.

A client who has done several of my programs has a big, juicy dream he's picked up and set back down several times. He recently had an epiphany in understanding who he is and why what he's up to matters. He sees that it's better to give his goal his best shot and miss than to get to the end of his life and wonder "What if?"

He said, "The area that continues to serve me most consistently is … connecting on a regular basis with my 'higher self' in order to achieve my goals. Developing my ability to slow my day down and to unify with what is in my heart is a life tool that I will forever use."

He's now solidly on track to achieve his goal. He dove headlong into his obsession and he's happily up to his ears in designing and building his Sexy Second Act. That's focus.

- surrounding yourself with like-minded people who support you and whom you support in return.

You have fierceness within you, whether you believe it or not. The world needs your ferocity and passion more than ever now.

What do you care about? What would you like to see change for the better?

There are a gazillion problems that need tackling. GMOs, starving children, global warming. You name it.

You have a choice. You can stand on the sidelines and complain. You can rant on social media. Or you can put on your fierce warrior gear, be willing to put your butt on the line, and take action about something that matters to you.

Either way, you are going to die someday. Do you want to be remembered as a hater or spectator? Or would you rather be remembered as a fierce doer and sexy difference-maker?

FOCUS

I grew up believing that discipline was either about punishment or hard work. Either way, it was distasteful to me. To this day, I prefer the word "focus."

I read somewhere that you must be willing to dive headlong into the depths of your obsessions. That's a pretty good way to look at focus. Diving headlong into the depths of your obsessions eliminates distraction and keeps everything clear and simple.

It's challenging to stay focused these days, with so many things demanding your attention. Here are some tools to include in your Focus Toolkit:

- Dive headlong into a big, juicy, exhilarating dream you are willing and eager to pursue.
- Determine why it matters.
- Choose a direction in the form of a goal. Like Yogi Berra said, "If you don't know where you are going, you might wind up someplace else."

Other focus tools include meditation; setting intentions; creating vision boards; hiring a coach; joining a mastermind group; and creating a mission or purpose statement.

A client who has done several of my programs has a big, juicy dream he's picked up and set back down several times. He recently had an epiphany in understanding who he is and why what he's up to matters. He sees that it's better to give his goal his best shot and miss than to get to the end of his life and wonder "What if?"

He said, "The area that continues to serve me most consistently is … connecting on a regular basis with my 'higher self' in order to achieve my goals. Developing my ability to slow my day down and to unify with what is in my heart is a life tool that I will forever use."

He's now solidly on track to achieve his goal. He dove headlong into his obsession and he's happily up to his ears in designing and building his Sexy Second Act. That's focus.

"F" Remodeling Techniques:

- Pick your favorite "F" word from this chapter as your theme for the day or week. Write it down and keep it with you.

- Use your "F" word in conversation. Share with someone what it means to you. Ask what it means to them. Write down any insights that open up.

- Take at least one action consistent with the word you chose.

- Does an "F" word that's not on this list resonate with you? Write it down and do the exercises on this page with the word you chose.

- Write down some examples of times you've failed. What did you learn? How did those experiences help you grow?

- Pick a goal to focus on fiercely. What focus tools will you put into practice to help you achieve it?

GAP

After years working in a corporate job, I would have given almost anything to escape for a year. Not because I didn't like my job. But because I felt burned out, and I wanted a break to recharge my batteries.

That kind of break used to be called a "sabbatical." Author Marc Freedman, who writes extensively about finding meaningful work in the second half of life, refers to it as a "gap" year. I like that term. It refers to both time and space … time to explore, and the space to do it in.

After years of dedicated work, the notion of taking a temporary "time-out" didn't seem like too much for me to ask. I dreamed of travel on my terms. I longed for free time to chill and do whatever I pleased. I envisioned sleeping in, taking long walks on the beach, going to the gym whenever I wanted, and trying out hobbies I'd always wanted to take up but never had time for. There were days when the thought of waiting for retirement to do those things made my heart ache, but at the time, I didn't think I had any other choice.

You know what they say, "Be careful what you wish for." The Universe apparently grew weary of listening to my silent prayer and decided to give me a good swift kick in the butt. Rather than granting me a sabbatical, She put me on leave of absence—permanently!

I wasn't too happy about this unplanned "gap" in the beginning. After thirty-plus years in the same company, dealing with my fear and anxiety about the future wasn't easy. I was laid off in early 2002 when many companies were down-sizing after September 11th. Not only that, many companies implemented a hiring freeze. I felt like I was staring into a huge, scary abyss where I would end up never earning an income again.

I had heard friends and colleagues say that getting fired or laid off was the best thing that ever happened to them. I didn't believe them. It wasn't until I experienced it myself that I learned they were right.

The drawback of spending your entire career in one place is that it tends to "silo" you. As I explored and grappled with what I was going to do next, my eyes were shocked wide open by just how drastically the world of work was changing.

Like it or not, we are now a global society, thanks to technology and social media. Like it or not, things are never going to be like they were before. Like it or not, you can't afford to put your head in the sand.

Those who use a "gap" to grow and adapt will thrive. Those who live in denial will struggle. No matter your age, it's important to stay flexible. And I don't mean just in your body, although that's an excellent idea.

Keeping up with the pace of change is daunting. But it's also exciting! There are limitless opportunities to explore based on what you love and find meaningful. You have the opportunity to invent a way to make every day a brand new adventure.

Take a good look around you. How many of your coworkers and associates look, feel, and act excited and energized on the job?

Look in the mirror. How excited and energized do you look, feel, and act? Do you notice a difference in your energy and excitement when you are about to leave on vacation versus after you've been back to work for a few weeks?

Routine dulls your spirit, drags down your energy, and stifles your creativity. Gaps, or time-outs, snap you out of your day-to-day rut. Used wisely, they bring you back to life and reinvigorate your spirit.

Whether or not you leave your job voluntarily, it's worth hitting your internal "pause button," no matter how uncomfortable it makes you feel. Give yourself a chance to meander through the gap rather than hurrying to "close" it or "fill" it.

Humans are creators. Creators need variety. Creativity can only show up when you slow down. Relax. Dream awhile. Recharge your batteries. Explore things you haven't made time for.

As you meander through the gap, you might thump up against obstacles like these:

- You have no idea what else you could do to make you a living or how to make money from doing what you love.
- You don't have enough money to give you the freedom to do things you want to do.

- You believe your family and friends will think you have gone completely off the rails. They may withdraw their support at the time you want it most.
- You think you don't have enough time to invent a brand new life.
- You don't have enough (or the right kind) of education.

Embrace the obstacles. They are there to help you grow and prepare for designing and building your Sexy Second Act. Be curious about ways to overcome them.

Get a mentor or a coach. Brainstorm. Mind map. Play with ideas. Move them around like puzzle pieces until you achieve that eureka moment when they fall into place.

Here is what is likely to happen as you explore your way through the gap:

1. You'll bring new ideas and a refreshed perspective to your current job upon your return.
2. You may discover that you love your job after all. You just needed a "time-out" to restore your energy.
3. By pulling your attention away from constantly running on autopilot, you get back in touch with parts of yourself you've lost sight of.
4. You get a glimpse of new horizons and points of view for designing the kind of meaningful career and life that's worthy of pursuing.
5. You get excited about what's possible.

Don't let obstacles kill off whatever crazy-ass-bodacious ideas you come up with for a future that makes your heart beat fast with anticipation. Use your time-out to create a blueprint for building your Sexy Second Act.

Don't worry if what you choose to pursue during your gap space seems silly. Travel if you love it. Take classes, even if you think they are off-the-wall. Basket Weaving or Banjo 101 may not land you your dream job, but a fun class or two will wake up your creative juices and your sense of play and fun.

Whatever you choose to explore is an opportunity to network. You never know who you'll meet that can lead you to your dream job or business.

The point is to make good use of your time-out. Stay curious about what exciting and fun Sexy Second Act you can design that captures your attention and amps up your energy. Set some goals. Take action. Even tiny steps can lead to extraordinary outcomes.

If you don't feel like you are in a position to ask for a sabbatical, you can still set aside time in your schedule for dreaming and scheming. The energy boost from giving yourself something to look forward to will keep you moving forward even if you are currently in a job you hate.

And you just never know. While you're dreaming, Sassy Serendipity just might waltz in with a sexy opportunity! That's her favorite thing to do. It might even show up exactly where you are. So keep your ears, heart and eyes wide open.

GENEROSITY

I left home one Sunday afternoon to run an errand. Since it was going to be quick, I didn't bother to grab my cell phone on my way out.

Two miles later, as I was about to make a left-hand turn, my car died. Completely. No radio, no flashers, no interior lights. Nothing. And no cell phone to call for assistance.

Being stuck in a left-hand turn lane does not endear you to your fellow drivers, who are rushing to run their own errands. I got plenty of dirty looks, finger signs, and honking horns as they maneuvered around me.

While I sat there wondering what the heck to do, a man appeared at my driver's side door. He asked if I needed help. He generously loaned me his cell phone to call a tow truck.

He offered to stay with me until the tow truck showed up, but I told him I'd be fine. I didn't want to take up more of his time. He said he needed to go to the store, but would check on me on his way out. I asked him for his business card, but he waved me off, and left to run his errand.

About ten minutes later the tow truck showed up. While I waited for my car to be hooked up, the man who had stopped to help me drove past, waved, and went on his way. I think he'd been waiting in his car in the parking lot to make sure I was taken care of.

Generosity is a hero who shows up in a baseball cap, T-shirt and jeans, and doesn't get annoyed by a stranger who has run into a problem. Instead, he stops to help and waits to make sure you're OK.

You can bet Mr. Generosity popped to the top of my gratitude list that night. It will be a long time before I forget his kindness. My wish for him is that he went to bed that night with a smile on his face, knowing he made a difference for a stranger in distress.

We don't practice the art of generosity enough these days. Look at any article posted online. You won't have to scroll very far through the comments before you see mean, ugly remarks.

We are even more malicious to ourselves than we are to each other. Before

Mr. Generosity showed up, my first reaction was to beat myself up for not taking my cell phone with me. What was I thinking? How stupid was that? I should know better ... yada-yada.

But then I caught myself. Nothing good comes from surrendering to negative self-talk. It certainly wasn't going to solve my problem. I would have panicked if I had allowed myself to keep tumbling down that rabbit hole.

I chose to be generous with myself. The situation was what it was. After all, things could have been worse. It could have been two o'clock in the morning rather than two o'clock in the afternoon.

I took a couple of deep breaths and pictured a good outcome. Perhaps a policeman would happen by. Perhaps someone else would call for help. Perhaps my car would miraculously start up. A couple of minutes after I started doing my good-outcome-picturing, Mr. Generosity showed up.

True generosity is humble. Mr. Generosity chose not to identify himself even though I would have loved to follow up with a thank you note and perhaps a gift card.

It's OK, though. I'm pretty sure the Universe has got this. Since everything that goes around comes around, his kindness is sure to be recognized, and he'll get a big dose of extra credit when She returns his kindness back to him.

Bona fide badass generosity comes from your heart. People know it when you're being generous for reasons of your own, like if you want to look good in your own eyes vs. in the eyes of others.

The next time you want to speak or act unkindly toward yourself or someone else, pause for a minute. What can you do to be generous instead?

It all comes down to how you want to be remembered and what you want to come back to you. Do you want to be thought of as a troll? Or would you rather be remembered with a smile as Mr. Generosity will be remembered every time I think about him?

GOALS

English writer Joseph Addison said there are three grand essentials to happiness in life: something to do, something to love, and something to hope for. I prefer to characterize the three grand essentials as something to do, something to love, and something to look forward to.

When you get right down to it, beyond taking care of the basics, money is not what most people are after. When you dream about winning the lottery, you aren't picturing the outcome as having big stacks of greenbacks lying around everywhere. You are dreaming about how you'd like to use those big stacks of money.

Money represents an experience you want to have. You are "wired" to have particular experiences or you wouldn't desire them. They resonate with you for a reason. Clarifying what kind of experiences you want to have is where you begin custom-designing and building your life your way.

If you can name the experience, you can claim it. One of my courses, January Jumpstart, focuses on creating goals. Almost everyone puts travel on their "hot" list of possibilities to pursue. Saying "I want to travel" isn't nearly as juicy as saying "I want to experience wanderlust," or "freedom to fly," or "bold adventure." Once you clarify the experiences you want to have, goals show up naturally and give you something to look forward to.

Want to be boldly adventurous? Maybe your Big, Juicy Goal (as I like to call it) will be to go skydiving, swim with the sharks, or para-motor through the Grand Canyon.

Big, Juicy Goals excite you down to the very core of your being. When you dream about them, they feel real. If your wanderlust dream is to sail around the world, you feel the wind in your face, taste the salty air on your tongue, and feel the deck pitching under your feet each time you dream about it.

To keep your enchantment, excitement, and joie-de-vivre alive, be specific about your dream. Start the energy flow of manifesting your dream into reality by surrounding yourself with symbols that represent it.

What kind of sailboat would satisfy your wanderlust dream? Hang or post pictures of it. Go to boat shows. Take a sailing class or join a sailing club. Talk to people who have done what you want to do. Jot down insights and ideas.

Make a list of what you need to take with you. Create a budget. Plot a route. Where would you stop along the way? Would you take someone with you or go it alone? Dream it any way you want it.

Of course Big, Juicy Goals take resources to accomplish, including your attention, time ... and money. People tend to focus on money—or the lack of it—and they stop giving their goals time and attention.

Focusing on lack is boring and unsexy. It drains your energy and will never get you where you want to go. Your committee is likely to jump in and tell you all the reasons you can't be, do, or have what you want.

It's acceptable to listen to what it says. But, treat what the committee tells you as a caution light, not as a stoplight. Its job is to help you survive. Caution means slow down. Look both ways before you proceed. Prepare. Make sure you have the right tools including a good strategy and a set of empowering beliefs.

You may have to dig deep into your toolbox to find them. That's OK. You can make it be a fun and rewarding part of the building process.

When done this way, setting goals stops being a chore. The more you play, the more ideas you'll get and the more alive you'll feel.

Your enthusiasm will attract supportive people, resources, and opportunities. You'll look forward to celebrating your accomplishments each year and to setting even better Big, Juicy Goals for the upcoming year.

GROWTH

It's a law of nature that if you aren't growing, you are dying. If you aren't expanding, you are contracting. Nothing in nature stays static.

Back when age sixty-five was the mandatory retirement age, we took a coworker to lunch to celebrate his retirement. I was young enough at the time to be blown away by the fact that he had worked for the company longer than I had been alive. Retirement for me was still a lifetime away.

I teased him that if it was me retiring, I'd celebrate the next Monday morning by setting the alarm just so I could think about my poor coworkers who had to be up and at 'em at o-dark-thirty. Then I'd smile, turn over, and go back to sleep.

He was not amused. Rather than chuckling like I thought he would, he looked at me oddly and didn't respond.

Within a month of retiring, he died. I was shocked. He hadn't been ill. A close friend of his told me that this man's job was his whole life and he hadn't really wanted to retire.

I've often wondered if he experienced his retirement as what author Steven Pressfield calls an "all is lost" moment. That's a rock-bottom moment when something inside you knows and believes you have no choice but to grow or die.

Did he see retirement as an ending rather than a chance for a new beginning? It made me sad to think so.

Without knowing it, he left me a legacy. I declared to myself that when my retirement came, I would make sure I had something new to look forward to. I vowed that I would prepare to have a meaningful life after my career was finished.

I was too young to know what that would look like. But the seeds were sown.

To grow, you must let go of the past. Like a snake shedding its skin, you must shed old ways of being, thinking, and behaving that no longer work. You must be willing to grow yourself into a new skin of possibility.

Sure, that can seem intimidating. You may start out feeling uncomfortable and awkward in your new skin. But if the only choices are growing or dying, choose growth. Growing makes life colorful, exciting, sexy, and fun!

"G" Remodeling Techniques:

- Pick your favorite "G" word from this chapter as your theme for the day or week. Write it down and keep it with you.

- Use your "G" word in conversation. Share with someone what it means to you. Ask what it means to them. Write down any insights that open up.

- Take at least one action consistent with the word you chose.

- Does a "G" word that's not on this list resonate with you? Write it down and do the exercises on this page with the word you chose.

- Look for a way to be generous in a way you wouldn't normally consider. For bona fide, badass points from the Universe, do it anonymously.

- Make a list of your Big, Juicy Goals. Pick one goal from your list. What experience does it represent? What is one action you can take toward achieving it right away? Take that action.

H

HEART

Research is discovering that our hearts generate a considerably stronger magnetic field than the magnetic field generated by any other organ in our bodies. More communication travels from our hearts to our brains than the other way around. Our hearts send a steady stream of intuitive information to our brains.

Research suggests that when our hearts and minds operate coherently, it positively impacts our health. Our immune system functions better. We are relaxed and creative. And yet, we let our brains override all but a fraction of the information sent by our hearts.

Why do we stop paying attention to what our heart wants? Perhaps we lose faith in our heart once it's been broken. We trusted and got hurt and so we vow never to let our heart be vulnerable again.

All this protecting and withholding produces poor results. It keeps you surviving, not thriving. It's no fun living a voiceless, heart-stunted, closed-up life.

My parents told me I was quite precocious when I was preschool age. We lived in a small town and, according to them, I made friends with everyone who passed by our house. I knew people they didn't know.

Being social worked until first grade when I got teased and bullied by older kids on the playground. Nothing like this had ever happened to me before. I had always been protected and treated with love, especially by adults.

The adults at school told me I had to fight my own battles. How does a smaller-than-average kid in first grade with no "street smarts" stand up to big kids eleven and twelve years of age? I had no clue. So I figured something must be wrong with me.

Painful childhood experiences lead us to conclude that there is something wrong about us. Because we don't know any better, we believe or misinterpret what adults tell us. We suppress the pain and live out the conclusion we jump to. We figure out a way to operate that covers up what we think is wrong until we do the work to untangle it from our subconscious memory.

I made up a story that "big kids are scary." As I grew older, big kids included adults in authority, even bosses and other people of influence.

My formerly open heart shut down, and I became wary of everyone. I yearned for love and connection, but I lived in terror of being hurt if I opened myself up. I trapped myself inside a prison of chronic, anxiety-riddled, living-life-in-black-and-white depression.

My personal get-out-of-jail card came decades later in the form of an epiphany. When I finally realized I had created a "limiting belief" called "big kids are scary," it was liberating. I'd made something up that was bullshit when I was too young to know better! And now I could let it go. What a relief!

Yeah, it was painful to see how much life I'd wasted living out my bullshit story. But letting it go freed me up to reconnect with what my heart wanted! My life has never been the same. Thank goodness!

What does your heart really want? What bullshit "limiting beliefs" have you made up to keep you imprisoned?

Take a good look. Do you worry about what others will think? Do your heart's desires seem silly and frivolous to your brain? Do you feel like you don't deserve the life of your dreams?

The truth is that what your heart authentically wants is never frivolous. Your heart's desires are meant to serve the world and fulfill you.

As Rumi, a 13th Century scholar, says, "Your heart knows the way. Run in that direction." Pay attention when your heart sings because sing, it does. Listen and design your life around the music and magic of its sexy song.

HEAVEN

I don't pretend to have the slightest clue about Heaven. But I ponder on it, occasionally. I doubt it's anything like we think it is or have been told it is. I suspect it's going to be far better and way more surprising.

Writer Ann Lamott says that sometimes she thinks Heaven is just a new pair of glasses. I'm down for a Heaven like that because, honestly, I don't want to go to a place where I get all the answers. I want a Heaven where there is both clarity and mystery.

I sometimes wonder if we model Heaven and Hell with our actions here on earth. Hell is what we put ourselves through when we resist or get scared. It's painful. We suffer. We cause others to suffer. We have "all-is-lost" moments. That's the dying part.

If we have the willpower to stay with it and work through our feelings of anger and fear, we have epiphanies that take us out of Hell and put us on the path to Heaven. Heaven is where love lives. Love allows us to see what we have been blind to.

Heaven is letting go of our limited view of ourselves and life. With a new pair of glasses, we emerge into a new view of the wonder, majesty, and beauty of the present moment and an expanded view of the future. Talk about a spectacular vista!

If you feel like you are living in Hell, it may be because you've got limiting beliefs or a poor strategy blocking your path to Heaven. Isn't it time to try on a sexy new pair of glasses and head down the path to a spectacular Heaven filled with fabulous fun and fulfillment, right here on Playground Earth?

HUSTLE

One day a friend and I were having a business discussion about ways to support another friend whose business was in trouble. In the end, my friend believed it would be impossible for us to help our other friend because she wasn't willing to hustle.

What he said resonated with me. There's a distinction in my mind between hustle and hard work. We couldn't help our friend because she saw her business as mostly hard work and a struggle to survive.

Hustle has a completely different energy to it than working hard does. Hard work means too many hours, too much stress, and stacking more and more and more on your plate until you buckle under the weight.

Ugh! Thinking about hard work immediately makes me want to take a nap. Hard work is no damn fun!

Hustle, on the other hand, sounds interesting and exciting. It sounds like dancing. It sounds like making fun things happen.

Hustle is about placing only those things on your plate that you want to do because they matter, they are healthy, and they taste good. It's about portioning what you put on your plate and not overloading it.

What you do may be the same, but your attitude about doing it is different when you are doing something you care about doing. You do it one bite at a time with focus and intensity because you are in the zone and happily engaged.

Hustle is about making a lot of mistakes, learning from them, and using what you've learned to grow. You are committed to doing what it takes to overcome roadblocks standing between you and designing your Sexy Second Act.

I recently spoke to someone who thinks he's too old at age forty-something to start something new. Seriously? These days that is barely even middle age!

He has at least twenty years before he reaches retirement age. If he stays healthy, he could have twenty or thirty years of active contribution beyond that. That's plenty of time to design and build something new, engaging, and wonderful.

He may just be tired and need a gap year to recoup his energy. Or perhaps he's afraid or thinks he hasn't got it in him to start over. That's a bullshit limiting belief. And it's a long way from bodaciously badass thinking!

Starting something new at forty-, fifty-, sixty-something or beyond, isn't about age. It's about hustle. Hustle is about action … right action!

Hustle requires you to demolish the box you've put yourself in to custom-design a way to work that fits your needs, desires, and life stage.

Hustle means letting go of your usual way of thinking about work. You just might come up with a dream life design that keeps you happily hustling for many years to come!

"H" Remodeling Techniques:

- Pick your favorite "H" word from this chapter as your theme for the day or week. Write it down and keep it with you.

- Use your "H" word in conversation. Share with someone what it means to you. Ask what it means to them. Write down any insights that open up.

- Take at least one action consistent with the word you chose.

- Does an "H" word that's not on this list resonate with you? Write it down and do the exercises on this page with the word you chose.

- Each time you have a decision to make, close your eyes and take a deep breath to quiet your mind. Focus your attention on your heart. Feel its powerful energy field surrounding you as you ask what it wants for you in this situation. If you feel "light-hearted" about the answer you get, you'll know you are onto something.

- Pick something that feels like hard work to you. What makes it important to the quality of your life? Play with ways to turn it from hard work into hustle.

I

IDEA

You can't imagine how many phenomenal ideas you have, and dismiss, without consciously being aware of them. I once heard author and speaker Mark Victor Hansen say that each of us has at least a single million-dollar idea. Ideas are bodaciously badass-sexy-cool because they are free, and limited only by the scope of your imagination and creativity.

Ideas are fickle little critters, though. You must learn to take care of them. If you don't pay attention to them, they scamper off to look for someone who is ready, willing and able to nurture them, cherish them, and coax them into manifesting into something delicious, fun, and wonderful.

The worst thing you can do with ideas is let them roam freely around in your head unsupervised. They are extremely talented escape artists. They refuse to stay put if you don't capture them by writing them down or recording them.

The sexy-cool thing is that ideas don't mind being captured. They float around craving to be grabbed up and brought into reality. They seem to play a little game with each other, competing to see which human will capture which idea.

What do we do instead of capturing them? We censor them. We judge them. We ridicule them. We think we aren't good enough for them or we think they aren't good enough for us.

The sad fact is that we too often listen to advice from people who are afraid to act on their own ideas. Yet they are happy to tell us, in excruciating detail, why our ideas are crazy or impractical or why they are doomed to fail.

If you were an idea, how long would you hang around if someone spoke about you like that? I don't know about you, but I'd run as fast as I could to a place I was wanted, and away from where I felt invalidated.

Trust your heart. Capture your ideas in an Idea file. Once they float away, you will have a tough time getting them back, if you get them back at all.

Keep your Idea file handy. Play with your ideas like you'd play with Legos® or building blocks. You never know when your curiosity and creativity will bring two seemingly unrelated ideas together in a brand-new way to form something wonderful and unique. That's when you'll be energized to hustle, no matter how much you are putting on your plate.

Ideas that make you buzz with excitement are designed by the Universe as a gift to you. You are meant to joyfully uplift and serve others with that gift.

Let go of ideas that don't energize you. They are meant for someone else. Keep the ones that excite you and delight you, even if they seem crazy or don't make sense at first.

Take action on your juicy ideas, even if it's only to share it with a trusted friend or advisor. No matter how off-the-wall-weird you think your idea is, go forward. Play freely. Make adjustments as you go.

You'll find out soon enough whether your idea will work. If it does, keep going. If it doesn't, you'll have learned something that may lead you to an idea that takes you to greater heights than you ever dreamed.

If you snooze, you lose. You know what I mean if you've seen a product or service and thought to yourself, "I had that idea years ago!" That's proof enough that ideas will move on to someone who will love, nurture, and act on them.

And then there's our impish friend, Serendipity, who loves it when you act on an idea. Her favorite thing is to wave her magic wand and deliver you a sweet surprise that will knock your socks off just when you least expect it. If that doesn't put a sexy smile on your face, nothing will!

INTEGRITY

While the dictionary defines integrity as a "state of being complete or whole," I prefer my friend Willy's definition. He defines integrity as "being solid with myself." That says it in a simple, straightforward, and elegant way.

You can be solid with yourself in one area of your life and not in another. A friend of mine is solid with herself regarding her marriage. When she declares that she and her hubby are going to the grave together, you hear the certainty in her voice. No bravado. No ego. Just solid certainty.

They've hit tough times in their marriage, as any couple does. But when those times come, there's no question they do what it takes to work through it. Sometimes they work through it on their own. But they aren't afraid to ask for assistance when they need it. Either way, they turn toward each other to work things out rather than give up or turn inappropriately toward someone else outside the relationship.

No one I know of is solid with themselves in every area of their lives all the time. That's probably not even possible in our human condition. Being solid with yourself means recognizing and owning areas where you lack integrity or fall out of it—and restoring it—as soon as you notice it.

As a busy working mom, my friend isn't always solid with herself when it comes to taking care of her own health and well-being. That doesn't mean there is anything wrong, or that she needs to beat herself up. She recognizes it as an area for growth and development. That's integrity.

The Top Five Regrets of the Dying by Bronnie Ware provides great examples of people looking back at the end of their lives and seeing places where they have not been solid with themselves:

- "I wish I'd had the courage to live a life true to myself, not the life others expected of me."
- "I wish I didn't work so hard."
- "I wish I'd had the courage to express my feelings."
- "I wish I had stayed in touch with my friends."
- "I wish that I had let myself be happier."

Being solid with yourself is bigger than keeping promises. It comes down to honoring who you are and treating the authentic part of you as sacred. Doing so may be the biggest challenge you face in your life because, first, you must recognize that there is a sacred self within you.

Honoring your sacred self makes you careful about what you give your word to. You'll stop compromising on things that matter. You'll stop giving your word to look good or be OK with others.

Author Carolyn Myss says that as we wake up, our choices become fewer, but they become much more powerful. You become charismatic and influential.

Your actions line up with the way you choose to live your life. You won't be lured away or distracted by "shiny" things. You become unstoppable in achieving your goals.

That level of integrity makes you solid with other people. They see you as being someone who is grounded, powerful, and who can't be messed with. They realize they can trust you to say what you are going to do and then to follow through on what you say.

The paradox about integrity is that while it's defined as having things be whole and complete, it's a game that's never finished for as long as you are alive. A simple way to look at it is that if something isn't working, feels off, or you feel powerless, look to see where integrity is missing and take responsibility for restoring it. Blaming something or someone is a way to avoid responsibility. Ask yourself:

- Are you in a job you hate? What's missing?
- Are you dissatisfied in your relationship? What's missing?
- Are your finances a mess? What's missing?
- Are you living an unhealthy lifestyle? What's missing?
- Are you feeling overwhelmed with too much to do? What's missing?

If you hate your job because the company culture honors profit and you honor the environment, it's out of integrity for you to stay. If you say "yes" to everything anyone asks you to do and you end up feeling exhausted, overwhelmed and resentful, it's out of integrity for you not to set boundaries on your time and energy. If you are dissatisfied in your relationship, it's out of integrity if you and your partner don't communicate to each other about what you each need.

You must be willing to hear and tell the truth about what's missing. This can be a challenge, but you can make a game of it.

Remember, it isn't about perfection, it's about excellence. As you become solid with yourself, you'll feel at home in your own skin. Your life will become interesting, engaging, happy, and workable. Being solid with yourself is downright sexy!

INTENTION

Whether you realize it or not, you intend constantly. The question is, are you intending consciously or unconsciously?

You can tell by what shows up in your life. The degree to which you like what shows up defines your personal level of effectiveness at consciously intending the life you want. Ask yourself:

- What are you intending when you say "I am sick and tired?" You may think you are intending to attract wellness and vitality, but where is your attention?
- When you say "I hate my job," you may think you are intending to attract a really great job that pays you well and supports your joy and creativity. But are you really setting yourself up for another day of misery?
- When you say "My [spouse/kids/mother-in-law/boss/neighbor] drives me crazy," you may think you are intending loving and nurturing relationships. But are you unconsciously designing another day of crazy-making drama?

The bad news is that it can be disconcerting to discover that you are in the driver's seat of what you create with your intentions, especially if you've been a poor driver. The good news is that you can learn to drive with the skill of a NASCAR racer.

If you've been unconsciously creating misery, chaos, and drama, you can change it in short order. All you have to do is consciously shift your attention toward what you want and away from what you don't want.

Think of intention as the starting line. It provides you with a direction in which to begin moving energy:

- I intend to live a life of amazing vitality, health, and well-being.
- I intend to work in an exciting, vibrant career with fun and creative

people, where my contribution is valued and appreciated.
- I intend to create intimate and warm family relationships where everyone feels loved, safe, and connected.

Your true intentions make you feel excited, happy, and inspired. Intention is the first step in moving energy toward manifestation.

Intending doesn't mean that you know how to make it happen. Trying to figure out the "how" will get you into trouble, big time. Don't go there. When you do, you'll stop good energy in its tracks, or you'll run your intentions off into a ditch.

Stay with the good feelings. Your brain is a bodaciously bad-ass problem solver if you put its attention in the right place. It will come up with possible actions you can take. If your goal is to get healthy and fit, your list might include joining a gym, giving up soda, going for walks with a friend, or signing up to train for a marathon.

Your job is to go with actions that intuitively feel the best. As you move in the direction of your intentions, you'll see more possible actions to take.

The Bible and other holy teachings offer us some sexy advice. "Ask, and it shall be given you; seek, and ye shall find; knock, and it shall be opened unto you."

Trust that advice and get thy butt in gear.

"I" Remodeling Techniques:

- Pick your favorite "I" word from this chapter as your theme for the day or week. Write it down and keep it with you.

- Use your "I" word in conversation. Share with someone what it means to you. Ask what it means to them. Write down any insights that open up.

- Take at least one action consistent with the word you chose.

- Does an "I" word that's not on this list resonate with you? Write it down and do the exercises on this page with the word you chose.

- Examine an area of your life that isn't working as well as you'd like it to work. Create an intention. Jot down possible actions. Check in with your heart. Take the action that intuitively feels right. What was the result?

- Pick an area of your life where something isn't working the way you'd like. What's missing in that area that would have it be joyful and fulfilling? What action can you take to put in what's missing? Take that action.

J

JELLO

You are probably thinking, "Ewww! Too much sugar! Why Jello?"

Sometimes words are nothing but fun. I say that if Disneyland is the happiest place on Earth, then Jello is the happiest food on Earth. Disneyland is sugary in its way, but no one says you shouldn't go there now and then.

Jello makes everybody smile. It wiggles and jiggles and dances and giggles its way through life. It wiggles and jiggles and dances like a puppy who's excited to see you after a long day of separation. We need more Jello in our lives.

We try so hard to plastic surgery, exercise, and nutrition our way out of jiggling and wiggling and dancing and giggling. The world might be a much better place if we lightened up, got a little bit sugary now and then and did stuff that had value for no other reason than it tasted good and gave us an experience of fun, play, and childlike joy.

Can you imagine a world where everyone happily wiggles and jiggles and dances and giggles to the tune of their own heart-songs? Holy giddy-asms, Batman!

Are you smiling yet?

JETTISON THE JUNK

Have you ever:

- Moved, opened up a packing box, and come across something that made you wonder why in the world you packed it?
- Put something in a junk drawer and later wondered what it was or realized that it belonged to something you had gotten rid of years before?
- Received a gift and put it away in a drawer to "save" for a special occasion that never came?

We humans are excellent hoarders, hanging onto stuff we don't need and will never use. We justify it by thinking we might need it "someday." We tell ourselves we are arming ourselves against some future potential calamity.

Before we know it, our closets and drawers are so full of clutter we can't find anything and there's no room to jam anything else in. There's no space left to bring in something fun and new.

These days we have the additional burden of digital clutter. How many email addresses do you have? Do you clear out your inbox every day, or do you have hundreds—if not thousands—of old emails cluttering up your digital space?

You never know. You might need that ten-year-old article on basket weaving someday.

We clutter up our minds, too. We clutter them with junk thinking, junk beliefs, and outdated crap that no longer serves us. And we rarely, if ever, take time to clear out the cluttered closets of our minds.

How much physical, mental, and emotional junk do you have stored up? Old beliefs. Resentments. Judgments. Gossip. Anything that happened in the past that you haven't let go.

Hanging onto all that stuff leads to stagnation. Stagnation is the death of creativity and your ability to design something new, stimulating and fun.

The cure is to declutter. Take inventory of what you are carrying around. Jettison the junk. Get rid of everything from your environment that you don't love. Jettison things you don't love doing. Jettison resentments, judgments, and gossip. Jettison people who suck you dry and disappear when you need their help or support.

When I was a kid, there were times when money was tight in our family. Despite their efforts to hide it, I remember my parents being afraid, and I could feel it.

I adopted the belief that money was scarce and that being without it is scary. I made up my mind that I didn't want to live being afraid about money. Somehow, I would make sure I had enough.

The good side of that decision is that I formed the habit of saving and investing early in my life. The downside was that I became a bit of a hoarder, hesitating to spend money on things I needed, wanted, and could afford.

I was driven to earn and save without stopping to identify specifically how much money it would take to feel "safe" financially.

Once I identified my limiting belief about scarcity, I could jettison it. I learned to set specific financial goals that feel good. Now that I have specific goals, I no longer live with a vague feeling of stress, anxiety, and worry about lack. Having a specific financial goal to go after is freeing.

Be willing to examine your beliefs and question them. How did you come to believe them? Are they yours as a result of your own experience, or have you adopted, without question, what your family or culture has taught you to believe?

Jettison everything that stands between you and living a joyful, fulfilling and relaxed life. Jettison it, even if you have to do it one drawer or one limiting belief at a time.

Be ruthless in cleaning up clutter. Remodel bit by bit until you are happily living the life that is simply and elegantly designed for you.

JOURNEY

I inherited my itchy travel feet from my dad. He'd done a considerable amount of adventuring as a young man and he had a way of captivating friends and family with his stories. His curiosity about new places and zest for new experiences infected me. I couldn't wait to grow up and have adventures of my own.

We went on family road trips as often as possible, sometimes for a day, other times for weekends. Our yearly vacations were almost always road trips. Our family could have been Chevy's ambassador for the 1950s' jingle "See the USA in your Chevrolet."

So far, my own adventures have included Australia, Tahiti, New Zealand, a bit of Europe and Asia, and a good portion of North America. Along the way, I discovered that there's a distinction between taking a trip and going on a journey.

A trip is merely a change in location. A journey, on the other hand, causes you to "demolish" and remodel your ideas and beliefs about the world, about people, even about yourself and your place in the world.

A journey takes you out of your comfort zone. You see things from a different perspective. Every culture has beautiful beliefs and traditions—if you take the opportunity to stay open and curious enough to learn about them.

On a journey, you have an opportunity to be an ambassador who listens and learns about people and culture and values. People respond to your genuine interest.

One of my favorite ambassadors, although he doesn't call himself that, is Matt Harding. His original goal was to journey around the world for six months. He shot videos of himself doing a funny little dance at various locations and he posted them on YouTube.

His videos caught on. People loved them, started following his adventures, and then started asking, "Where the heck is Matt?" He created a blog documenting his travels.

In later videos, people around the world were inspired to meet up with Matt and dance along with him. Everyone looks happy. His travels created a community of smiling people having a wonderful time dancing together.

Matt could not have predicted that recording himself doing a funny little dance would inspire people the way it did. He may have started out taking a trip, but he ended up taking a journey, becoming a motivational speaker, and sharing his stories.

You can transform your life by immersing yourself in a journey, whether it's traveling the globe or exploring your inner world. Journeys connect you to the world, to yourself, and to your roots.

If your life has gotten stale and stagnant, bring yourself back to life by going to a place you've never been. As T. S. Eliot said:

> *"We shall not cease from exploration And the end of all our exploring Will be to arrive where we started. And know the place for the first time."*

JOY

Joy is one of my personal guiding principles. I define it as experiencing the world with childlike wonder.

What would the world be like if we greeted each new day with childlike wonder? What's going to happen today? Why is the sky blue? What new game can we play? What's that? Who's that? Where are we going? What fun thing are we going to do?

Little kids show up for life without any preconceived notions about how it "should" go. They spread their arms wide and joyfully greet each day as a brand-new adventure. They don't worry about how they look or what anyone else thinks. They are ready to play.

That little kid still exists inside of you. You can access your own sense of childlike wonder by suspending your judgment about how life "should" go. Be willing to play with your dreams.

What brings you joy? What would joy look, feel, taste, smell, and sound like if you could have it exactly your way? What elements of that experience can you bring in right away? What kind of "remodeling" plan can you come up with to add more joy bit by bit by gleeful bit until you tingle from head to toe?

JUMP

I believe your juiciest dreams pursue you throughout your life. If you don't accept the call to make them come true, you will be left with a hole in your heart where that dream fits.

Skydiving was that kind of dream for me. I both wanted to do it and was terrified of doing it. I kept putting it off.

Until I met a fifty-something grandmother in a course I coached. She was shy and quiet and she didn't share much about herself. She faced a number of major challenges in her life and in her marriage.

When a group of participants got the idea for going skydiving, she decided she wanted to go along. Her big "why" for going skydiving was to become a role model to her grandchildren.

Skydiving turned her into a different person. Gone was the shy, withdrawn, and quiet woman who kept everyone at bay. Her face lit up with joy as she walked proudly to the front of the room to share her experience. She held up a super-sized photo of herself soaring high above the ground. The smile on her face outshone the sun.

The entire room sat spellbound as she shared how she discovered courage she didn't know she had and how she intended to use that courage to create a different life for herself. By the time she finished describing what skydiving was like for her, the rest of us were ready to jump!

Best of all, she shared how proud her grandson was of her. He couldn't wait to tell his school classmates how cool his grandma was. He had to show her photo to his class before the teacher and his classmates would believe that his grandma had really done it!

After hearing her story, I knew that next time I had the opportunity, I would jump. I wasn't sure it would have such a huge impact on me, but I learned that there's only one thing to do when your heart calls you. Jump and "let the wind take you."

You may not understand the purpose of it until after you make the jump, but that's where faith comes in. Jumping when it feels scary, uncomfortable, or uncertain is meant to grow you and give you the greatest experience of who you are and what you are capable of accomplishing.

Nothing makes you feel more vibrant and alive than jumping into something that calls to your heart. It's exhilarating. It makes you feel like a winner who is ready to take on the next challenge. And the one after that. Before you know it, you become your own champion. Is that sexy or what?

"J" Remodeling Techniques:

- Pick your favorite "J" word from this chapter as your theme for the day or week. Write it down and keep it with you.

- Use your "J" word in conversation. Share with someone what it means to you. Ask what it means to them. Write down any insights that open up.

- Take at least one action consistent with the word you chose.

- Does a "J" word that's not on this list resonate with you? Write it down and do the exercises on this page with the word you chose.

- Pick at least one thing to "jettison." Notice how you feel afterward. Lighter? More free? What can you put into place to remind yourself to periodically jettison the junk in your life?

- Write down at least one dream or goal you've put on hold. What would it feel like to accomplish that dream or goal? What will it feel like if you never accomplish it? What action can you take now to accomplish your dream?

K

KALEIDOSCOPE

Did you have a kaleidoscope when you were a kid? Even now, can you resist picking one up and looking inside? It's such a delightful invention! Even the word sounds happy as it rolls off your tongue.

The dictionary says it comes from two words that translate to "beautiful shape." I like the notion of random bits of things coming together to form a beautiful shape.

A kaleidoscope is what I think of when I remember my dad and the group of friends he made after he retired and moved to a small town in Northern California. He gravitated to this group of friends because they didn't sit around complaining about being old. They played golf, traveled together, went to dinner, and partied at each other's houses.

And I do mean party! They could put many young people to shame with their shenanigans.

They reminded me of a kaleidoscope because they came together from a variety of places and backgrounds. Some had been rough-and-tumbled by life, like one couple who lost their only son in the Vietnam War. Others had led privileged lives. My dad's life experience fell somewhere in between.

The variety of their backgrounds didn't matter. By the time they had reached a certain age, life had leveled the playing field. They had survived. They no longer had time or energy to waste on petty squabbles. They knew how precious their remaining time was. They weren't about to waste it complaining about what they no longer had. They were too busy living full out in the moment.

They took care of each other when someone got ill or passed away. And when my dad passed, they took care of me.

Most of them are gone now. But memories and little pieces of their stories tumble in my heart like beautiful bits of brightly colored glass that I love looking at from time to time.

They taught me a few things about life:

KALEIDOSCOPE

- Don't take it so seriously.
- You're never too old to fall in love or to have a new adventure.
- When you get old, it's important to have good friends who take care of each other.

Do you have an older someone in your world you haven't paid attention to beyond the role they play in your life? A parent, grandparent, neighbor, coworker, or business associate? Their stories are colorful bits and pieces that eventually tumble into a beautiful shape called a life. By listening, you might discover something beautiful and exquisite that will help you appreciate and make the most of your own life's journey.

Your life is a colorful kaleidoscope. What has shaped you? How can you pass on what has shaped you to those you will leave behind one day? What will they think about when they see the kaleidoscope that is you?

K.I.S.S.

My variation on the K.I.S.S. axiom of "keep it simple, stupid" is "keep it simple … and sexy!"

Despite what people believe, keeping things simple does not mean keeping them stark, barren, and dull. Ugh! That is not sexy!

Simple means boiling things down to their elegant essence. What you love is simple. What you want is simple. Your purpose in life is simple.

That doesn't mean it's easy. For instance:

- Creating a vision of what you want is simple. Manifesting what you want will require you to stretch.
- Setting a goal is simple. Achieving goals worthy of your time will take you out of your comfort zone.
- Knowing your purpose is simple. Living it will test your commitment.

The challenge is what makes building a vision, pursuing a goal, or manifesting your purpose, sexy. You're discovering where your personal limits are and designing ways to break through them.

You won't get to choose all of your challenges, but you do get to choose how to respond to them. Boil each challenge down to its elegant essence. Ask yourself quality questions that help you hone in on the lesson, the next step, or the way to design a magnificent outcome.

When you get overwhelmed, it's likely that you've allowed yourself to collect too much clutter. That's when it's time to stop and tune in to the elegant essence of what really matters to you.

Do some housecleaning. Jettison the junk. Keep at it until you can breathe freely again. Breathing freely is sexy!

"K" Remodeling Techniques:

- Pick your favorite "K" word from this chapter as your theme for the day or week. Write it down and keep it with you.

- Use your "K" word in conversation. Share with someone what it means to you. Ask what it means to them. Write down any insights that open up.

- Take at least one action consistent with the word you chose.

- Does a "K" word that's not on this list resonate with you? Write it down and do the exercises on this page with the word you chose.

- Pick a challenge you are facing. What great questions can you ask yourself to simplify it down to its elegant essence?

Note: If you want examples of quality questions, you'll find some under the letter "Q."

L

LAUGHTER

There's nothing like a down-to-earth belly laugh to alter your state. It's such a giddy-licious release of stress! Laughter is infectious and connects us to each other in a way that few happy experiences do.

Kids laugh at least four times as often as adults. Where does our sense of fun disappear to when we grow up?

It's no secret that laughter has many health benefits. It boosts your immune system, lowers blood pressure, and releases endorphins. We know it's good for us, but we still don't laugh nearly often enough or boisterously enough.

I love those TV bloopers where the serious news anchor breaks up completely. Most TV news is so ridiculously disheartening that a good belly laugh is sorely needed now and then.

We'd be better off if we took life a lot less seriously. I once attended a girls' night out party where something got us laughing so hard we couldn't stop. All except for one gal, who just couldn't let herself go. The best she could do was muster up a slight smile. She couldn't give herself permission to laugh from deep in her belly.

She gave us reasons for why she couldn't really laugh. But the truth is that she was almost always tightly wound, serious, and proper.

Writer Anne Lamott says laughter is "carbonated holiness." I love that. I would add that a good belly laugh is champagne-giddy-tickle-your-nose holiness.

It's not easy to stand back and take a look at how wonderfully-messed-up-dingbat-crazy humans are. We don't like to admit it.

Sanity shows up when you can stand back, acknowledge, and appreciate how divinely, creatively, wildly and weirdly whacked out and wonderful you are. Then you can laugh compassionately at your own insanity and the insanity of humanity.

Our greatest comedians, like Robin Williams, Richard Pryor, and George Carlin were masters at poking fun at the delicious joke life is. Through them,

LAUGHTER

we recognized ourselves and our humanity. That recognition helps to release the grip our craziness has on us.

I recently saw a meme on Facebook that said, "Laugh till you leak." Oh yeah! That's a motto well worth adopting!

How often do you laugh? I don't mean the occasional chuckle, I mean a full-on belly laugh that leaves you shaking like jello, with aching cheeks, sore tummy muscles, and shortness of breath.

Laughter provides us with a delicious way to release toxic energy. What actions can you take to bring more belly laughs into your life?

LEAP OF FAITH

Every time you choose to do something without certainty about how it's going to turn out, you take a leap of faith. Even something as simple as getting behind the wheel of a car or boarding an airplane requires you to take a leap of faith.

You may not think of it that way it because you do it often enough that it's become automatic and doesn't seem extraordinary. But what you think of as ordinary would require a huge leap of faith for someone born a couple of hundred years ago.

A leap of faith is a conscious act. You take stock of the risks and you accept the consequences, regardless of how it goes. Activities like getting married, having a child, or starting a business require a leap of faith. There's no way to know for sure ahead of time how it's going to turn out.

A leap of faith goes deeper than getting married because society says it's what you are "supposed" to do. It goes deeper than starting a business because you want to have more free time. It goes deeper than having a child because you want a "mini-me" who will fulfill the dreams that didn't work out for you.

Leaps of faith are not careless acts. You don't call it a leap of faith to jump into matrimony before you find out enough about each other to know if you are on the same page financially or if you share similar goals. You don't call it a leap of faith to have a child if your spouse wants a kid and you don't. You don't call it a leap of faith to start a business if you haven't done the research to understand what you are getting into. That's potential suicide … to your finances, your well-being, and your relationships.

You take a leap of faith when you choose to do things that align with being true to yourself. You know somewhere deep inside that you have no other choice than to go for the dream that makes of your life everything it can possibly be. Leaps of faith require you to trust your inner voice, prepare as best you can, take a deep breath and "leap," knowing that you are ready to accept whatever comes.

When I was considering going skydiving, I wrote in my journal that there comes a time when something inside you tells you that you must "fly or die." Champion skydiver Dan Brodsky-Chenfeld describes it like this when he talks about his first skydive in his book *Above All Else*:

> *"All the dreaming about skydiving and talking about skydiving came down to this second ... if I ever wanted to fly like I always dreamed of flying, I was going to need to jump off this plane ... That moment of decision time is the essence of what is meant by taking a leap of faith."*

He said that whenever you go after a goal that stretches you, you have to trust that the world you are going to jump into will work out as it should.

Here's what I wrote in my journal after watching my skydiving video multiple times:

"I keep seeing that moment when my instructor and I jumped out of the plane. I can't believe that's me. I can't get over the feeling of what it's like to hurtle yourself out there and trust it will be OK ...It defies everything I 'know' about myself as someone who is fearful, incompetent and small."

When you take a leap of faith, you are putting something at stake for a compelling outcome. A compelling outcome for marriage might be love and partnership. A compelling outcome for starting a business might be to make the world better with your product or service. A compelling outcome of having a child might be the opportunity to nurture and develop a future generation of caring and compassionate human beings.

My leap of faith for skydiving was more than trusting I would reach the ground safely. It was a sense, deep inside, that it would lead to a breakthrough in my personal growth. The compelling outcome was that skydiving changed my relationship to fear. Since then, whenever I encounter something that scares me, I remind myself that if I can jump out of an airplane, I can do anything.

Leaps of faith are sexy game changers. When you take one, you are jumping into a new paradigm where you experience who you are in a whole new way. Your leap of faith may not turn out exactly like you want it to. More often than not, it turns out better.

Do you have a persistent dream living inside you? There's a reason it keeps calling you. You may not know the reason until after you take a leap of faith to accomplish it.

Trust yourself and jump. No matter how it turns out, you won't ever have to wonder about what could have been. Having no regrets is bodaciously badass sexy.

LEGACY

Leaving a legacy may be something you don't think very much about, especially if you are young. Time feels like it stretches out endlessly before you. You are busy dealing with the urgency of this phase of your life—making a living, dealing with relationships, and starting or raising your family.

It's generally later in life when you start to ponder the kind of legacy you want to leave. Will it be one that makes people glad you were here? Or will you leave one that makes people relieved you are gone?

I recently read a Facebook post about a group of friends who gathered together to conduct an "un-funeral" to celebrate one of them. They called it an un-funeral because the person being celebrated was still alive. The post didn't specify how this event came about, but I thought it was an intriguing idea.

Why wait for someone to depart before telling them how much they mean to you? It's insane to wait until they are gone and can no longer hear it. Why not let them know the impact they've had on you while they are still alive? That's sexy!

While you are at it, why not find out the impact you have on others while you still can? You don't have to conduct an "un-funeral," although that could be bodaciously badass fun. You can get instant feedback by asking quality questions of people who matter to you:

- What's it like to be my friend, spouse, mom, child, sibling, or coworker?
- What can you depend on me for? (Or not depend on me for?)
- What annoys you most about me?
- If I could change one thing to make our relationship better, what would it be?
- What do I do that inspires you? (Or uninspires you?)

You can add your own questions to this list.

This might seem like a scary thing to do. And you are right. It takes courage. If you are brave enough to do this exercise, you might discover a gap between how you want to be thought of and how people actually think of you.

You may hear things you didn't count on hearing. Or, you might be surprised by how much of a difference you make in the lives of people who love you. You may have no idea of the ways in which you have touched people.

Take a leap of faith. Ask for honest feedback. Accept what you hear without defending yourself. Think of what the other person is saying as being something they observe about you. It's not necessarily the truth about you.

Be a detective. Look for clues about how you are perceived. Don't do anything at first but gather the clues. Like a good detective, listen without influencing what the other person has to say. You can analyze the clues and decide what to do with them later.

You'll get a feel for the kind of legacy you are generating. If you like what you hear, keep going. If you don't like what you hear, you have a choice to make about how willing you are to make conscious adjustments that lead to you being remembered exactly the way you want to be remembered.

I think it would be bodaciously badass sexy to leave the planet with a smile, already knowing what's going to be said about me at my funeral. What do you think?

LISTENING

Have you ever stopped to listen to someone with all of your senses? This level of listening is magnetic. People find you attractive and want to be around you. They feel appreciated and acknowledged in your presence.

According to Nancy Kline, author of *Time to Think: Listening to Ignite the Human Mind* (Ward Lock, 1999, p. 36), the ability to listen to another person without judgment, opinion, or thinking about how you will respond brings out their own intelligence and creativity. She says, "Giving good attention to people makes them more intelligent. Poor attention makes them stumble over their words and seem stupid."

Learning to listen with no agenda other than to listen is simple. But it's not easy. We think we listen, but we are actually trying to figure out:

- what's wrong with the other person's opinion and how to "win" and be right
- whether what's being said aligns with what we believe, know or understand
- how quickly we can interrupt, change the subject, or move the conversation along to a topic we find more relevant or interesting
- whether the other person sounds smarter, more educated, or cooler than we do, and if so, how we can avoid being "found out" if we feel like we are lacking
- what we are going to say in response.

We don't hear what's being said and we don't hear what's not being said. We don't pay conscious and respectful attention to body language, tone of voice, or how we feel about what they are saying or how we feel about being with them.

We don't pay much attention to our own thoughts, either. We allow them to run amok inside our head without observation, evaluation, or conscious intention.

Various sources indicate that we think upwards of twenty thousand thoughts a day. The problem is that we think the same thoughts every day.

We think we are thinking our own thoughts. But mostly, we are thinking thoughts from the past. They are thoughts given to us by our upbringing, religion, gender roles, and culture. No wonder people wander around looking like bored robots.

Sit in a mall or airport and watch people as they walk by. How many of them look excited? What do you think they are thinking? Yummy thoughts? Creative thoughts? Or same-old-same-old thoughts?

If you want to jumpstart your success, practice listening from your heart. Listen to yourself and others with all your senses, not just your ears. Listen with curiosity, openness, and compassion. Suspend your judgment and agendas, and just listen.

Give away powerful listening and you might just see magical things start to happen, especially if you are someone who doesn't feel heard. As a coach, I've experienced those times when a client thinks I've said something brilliant when the truth is, I hardly said anything and they were able to work something out on their own.

I love it when that happens. Magic is sexy!

"L" Remodeling Techniques:

- Pick your favorite "L" word from this chapter as your theme for the day or week. Write it down and keep it with you.

- Use your "L" word in conversation. Share with someone what it means to you. Ask what it means to them. Write down any insights that open up.

- Take at least one action consistent with the word you chose.

- Does an "L" word that's not on this list resonate with you? Write it down and do the exercises on this page with the word you chose.

- Think about times in your life when you trusted your heart and took a leap of faith. How did it turn out? What did you learn about yourself?

- Pick someone in your life to have a conversation with. Practice listening without interrupting. Give them complete freedom to say what's on their mind. Notice when you drift off to judge, compare, or think about how you want to respond. Write down any insights that occur.

M

MASTERMIND

There's an African proverb that says:

"If you want to go fast, go alone. If you want to go far, go together."

Masterminding is a term I first heard several years ago when I was trying to figure out how to design and build my own Sexy Second Act. The idea of masterminding excited me. It had never occurred to me that you could surround yourself with people who support your visions, dreams, and goals. Growing up as an only child, it was an experience I wasn't familiar with.

Masterminding is a powerful tool for moving your life forward way faster than you can do on your own. Why? Your mastermind partners:

- have access to helpful resources, and vice versa
- are knowledgeable in a variety of areas
- come up with ideas you haven't thought of yet
- have skills you don't have
- provide a great sounding board, offering you objective feedback about your ideas and goals.

Together, you and your mastermind partners can tap into more opportunities to quickly grow your businesses and your lives than any one member can do on their own. When you surround yourself with people who have your back and you have no doubt about it, ideas flow freely. Shared ideas act like sparks. Just one spark can ignite a firestorm of creative thinking in the other members. When everyone starts to play, creative solutions result.

Trust grows. You feel safe to share your successes and challenges. Mastermind members bond and begin to care about each other's results as much as they care about their own. Everyone takes ownership for the entire group's success. Lifelong friendships and business alliances are often formed.

Mastermind groups work when you are willing to:

- Be accountable.
- Trust and be trusted.
- Hold what members share in strict confidence.
- Be vulnerable.
- Ask for support.
- Give and take straight feedback.
- See the greatness in your fellow members and surrender to the greatness they see in you.

The world is changing so much and so quickly, there's just no way to keep up with all you need to know by yourself. Your mastermind partners keep you focused and grounded. Your meetings can be the eye of the hurricane, where you find peace and clarity amid today's environment of chaos and uncertainty.

Through facilitating mastermind groups, I've seen clients overcome major obstacles and accomplish Big, Juicy Goals they wouldn't have otherwise achieved. If you want to go fast, go alone. If you want to go far, go with others. If you want to go farther faster, put yourself in a mastermind group.

MIRACLE

The word "miracle" comes across to many people as new-age-airy-fairy. Or religious. You know, visions of water turning into wine and all that jazz.

I'm not saying miracles like that aren't possible. I wonder, though. Do we spend so much time looking for otherworldly miracles that we miss the "ordinary" ones that surround us every day?

Sunsets. Clouds. Roses. Redwood trees. Kid laughter. Love. Birdsong. Dog kisses. The wind in your hair. Friends. Bread pudding and whiskey sauce.

Miracles surround us. It's miraculous enough even to be alive. All manner of universal chaos could wipe us out in an instant. And yet, here we are. That alone is worthy of a daily double dose of gratitude.

And then there is the miracle of you. Wayne Dyer said that being starts with an idea. God had an excellent idea called you, and somehow, out of the mists of the Universe, a big batch of intelligent molecules got together and agreed to hang out and be "you" for a few decades.

The odds of you being born as you, exactly as you are, are about one in four hundred trillion. And you want to pooh-pooh the idea that you are a miracle? You dare to think you are not enough! That's pretty funny when you think about it.

Quantum Theory poses the idea that you are more space than you are solid. Assuming that's the case, don't you have to wonder what holds you together as you? How can you think of yourself as something other than the result of some mysterious and miraculous agreement at an intellectual level we can't begin to grasp?

I know, I know. I get it. You've rarely, if ever, been told you are a miracle. Instead, you've been told a bazillion times what's wrong with you. And you've told yourself the same thing a bazillion times more.

But seriously. Think about it. It doesn't matter if you believe you are here by some random coincidence or if you think you are here by Divine Intervention. You are here and that fact alone makes you a bodaciously badass miracle!

Stop wasting time trying to fix yourself! Make it your mission to find out what makes you happy and how you can contribute your joy to serve others. Then get into action doing that.

See yourself as God's excellent idea brought into reality. That's all you need to believe to accept that you are worthy of being, doing, or having all the good the Universe has in store for you.

Become unreasonable, unstoppable and 100% committed to putting your life on the line for something that matters to you. Your juicy life is at stake. Make it as big, badass, bold, and bodaciously sexy as you can!

You are a miracle capable of causing miracles. Allow yourself to believe it. You have big dreams, even if you don't yet know what they are. Be willing to uncover and go after them. When you do, you'll shine brighter than any star you see in the sky. You'll burn hot and sexy.

Yes, stars burn out eventually, and so will you. Do you want to burn out from exhaustion, or would you rather burn out like a supernova that lit the way for others?

How's that for an excellent legacy?

MONEY

You can't talk about creating a bodaciously badass Second Act without bringing up crazy, sexy money. People are willing to kill for it; lie, cheat and steal for it; or worst of all, start wars over it.

What could they accomplish if they directed their intelligence and creativity in a more positive direction? How many global problems could be solved in the span of a generation?

Instead, in pursuit of it, they demolish their lives and the lives of others. If that's not nuts, what is? Because what is money? Pieces of rag paper, bits of shiny metal, or carbon particles that, under pressure, turned into chunks of glittery glass. That's what we humans get wacked-out over.

Of course, our money wackiness has nothing to do with shiny metal, rag paper, or glittery glass. It's what it represents ... security, freedom, power and influence, independence, contribution, or having fun.

Your energy gives money its value and meaning. High energy, high return. Low energy, low return. Just like you can't build a quality house using poor-quality materials, you can't build a high-quality life with poor-quality energy.

The amount of money you have is a good indicator of the quality of energy you are expending. You get compensated in proportion to the kind of energy you are willing to expend creating value for others.

High-quality energy includes fun, curiosity, excitement, creativity, action, and being of service. Poor-quality energy includes negative thinking, drudgery, complaining, and staying stuck.

If you aren't generating the amount of money you want to generate, take a look at where you are focusing your attention. If it's focused on poor-quality energy, you are blocking abundance.

In his book *The Trick to Money is Having Some* (Hay House Australia, 1989, p. 56), Stuart Wilde says there are three kinds of abundance:

- Intellectual
- Emotional/Spiritual

- Physical/Commercial

Intellectual abundance is the easiest for you to tap into. You have education, skills, and ideas galore. You can garner more by reading books, searching the internet, taking classes, or masterminding. Your limitless intellectual capacity will help you design a good strategy for building your money house.

You may have to dig deep to tap into your emotional/spiritual abundance. If you don't yet have the amount of money you want, be willing to take a good, authentic look at what you believe about money.

Do you believe you aren't smart enough, creative enough, talented enough, or worthy enough to make enough money to support your Sexy Second Act life, business, or career? How do you "know" that's true?

Do you believe it takes a traditional college degree or job to make enough money to survive? Do you believe it's "too late" or that you've invested too much time and energy in your current field to switch careers and do what you love? How do you "know" that's true? Have you explored your options?

Do you believe that all the "good jobs" are going overseas and there are no opportunities left for you, especially if you are of a certain age? How do you "know" that's true? How do you know that there isn't a limitless field of opportunity awaiting your skills and abilities and hungry for your contribution if you are open to going in a different direction?

Limiting beliefs function like ghosts in the attic. You can't see them, but they haunt you, occasionally rattling their chains and scaring you. Be willing to hunt them down and exorcise them.

A friend recently uncovered one of her limiting beliefs about money—that men are "supposed" to earn it and give it to women. Nice gig if you can arrange your life that way and still retain your self-respect. But that's a tricky balancing act for both parties.

A client had been in a job she hated for more than ten years and felt stuck. I invited her to accompany me to a networking event attended primarily by small business owners. She had no idea there was such a variety of businesses and business opportunities.

A former client loves a particular sport, but cannot play professionally. He's "stuck" in his current job because he doesn't see a way he can use his skills and knowledge in a way that will support him.

Working through your limiting beliefs can be challenging and painful, but on the other side lies sexy, juicy freedom. The first step is to let go of what you "know" and open your eyes to possibility thinking.

Physical/commercial abundance is an outcome of the other two. Since leaving my job, I've associated with many people who dream of having successful businesses, but they somehow think it's going to happen without expending energy to hustle their way to success.

You can have talent, education, and ideas galore. You can believe in yourself up the wazoo. But if you don't take action and move energy, nothing is going to happen.

If you think the law of attraction is about something falling into your lap, you've got it wrong. It's only when you start moving energy that Serendipity starts peeking over your shoulder to see what you are up to.

I know leaps of faith are scary. When I get scared, I think about that scene in the movie *Indiana Jones and the Last Crusade* where Indy has to cross a chasm to get to the Holy Grail. He has to take a leap of faith that there's a bridge in front of him, even though it's invisible to the human eye.

He had the ingredients needed for success. He had a goal. He had a big why. He had a guidebook.

Still, he couldn't be sure. He had to take a leap of faith. He had to hustle to prevail over every obstacle he encountered.

In the end, he harvested the reward. You will, too.

"M" Remodeling Techniques:

- Pick your favorite "M" word from this chapter as your theme for the day or week. Write it down and keep it with you.

- Use your "M" word in conversation. Share with someone what it means to you. Ask what it means to them. Write down any insights that open up.

- Take at least one action consistent with the word you chose.

- Does an "M" word that's not on this list resonate with you? Write it down and do the exercises on this page with the word you chose.

- What are your money beliefs? That it grows on trees? That a penny saved is a penny earned? That time is money? Make a list of every cliché you can think of about money and the beliefs you inherited from your family. Write down any insights you have. How can you use your insights to create some sexy, juicy energy and freedom regarding money?

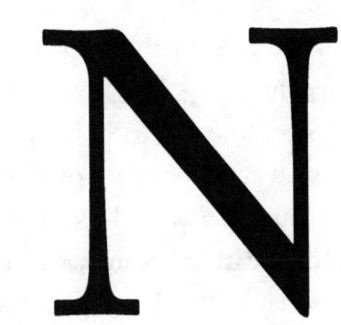

NO

What an interesting relationship we have with the word "no." We tend to overvalue it when we hear it from someone else, and undervalue saying it when it comes to setting boundaries around our own time, values, and priorities. Consider:

- How often do you give in to someone else's insistence or sense of urgency when you want to say "no"?
- How often do you avoid asking for what you want for fear of hearing "no" in response to your request?
- How many times do you do something you don't want to do to avoid hurting someone's feelings?

This humble two-letter word gets a boatload of extra meaning attached to it. Rejection. Disapproval. Denial. Go away. Talk to the hand.

Maybe we have a tough time with it because, according to experts, we are told "no" roughly 400 times a day in the first year of life or so. And when we were kids and told our caregivers "no," they often snapped at us for talking back. Or they overrode our "no" to protect us and, as kids, we just thought they were spoiling our fun.

Used properly, "no" is a powerful tool to keep in your toolbox. When you say "no" to something you don't want or to something that doesn't work for you, you are taking a stand for something important you do want.

Rosa Parks said "no" when she was asked to move to the back of the bus. She said "yes" to herself as being worthy of receiving dignity and respect. She said "no" to a system that didn't work. She said "yes" to her own integrity.

Look at how that one simple "no" ended up reverberating throughout our society! It ignited a movement.

Someone else's "no" doesn't diminish or devalue you or your request. They have their reasons for saying no that rarely, if ever, have anything to do with you, even if it doesn't feel good when you hear it.

NO

Your "no" doesn't diminish or devalue others. You show how much you honor and value them when you say "yes" only when you genuinely want to serve and contribute.

Learn to honor, respect, and value the word "no." It can be your ally, your friend, and your protector. Setting strong boundaries is totally sexy!

NOTHING

Very few words speak to the wonder of paradox like the word nothing—no-thing. Zip. Zero. Nada. No-thing except the possibility of everything. A blank canvas. A space from which to create whatever you want to create.

Holy teachings say that the entire Universe was created from no-thing. Wow! What a splendid imagination the Divine One has.

Those same teachings tell us that we are created in that image. We are magnificent creators with incredible imaginations who have the ability to manifest beautiful dreams and visions into reality from no-thing.

That's hard to remember when your world is falling apart—when you lose a job, the love of your life, your money, or your health. Everything feels uncertain and chaotic.

Destruction and chaos are a necessary part of creation. Reducing everything to no-thing gives you a fresh, blank canvas upon which to create.

What would be possible if you believed, without a doubt, that you have the power to create something fantastic and fulfilling and freeing and fun from a completely blank space of no-thing? Would it scare you or would you embrace it?

No matter what challenges you are facing, you can learn to bring yourself to a state of no-thing. No-thing to do. Nowhere to go. No-thing to fix. No thinking. Just being present, in the moment.

When you arrive at your no-thing space, you open a space for something wonderful to appear. New ideas, new possibilities, new synchronicities.

Nearing your no-thing space can seem scary at first. Things you haven't wanted to look at or deal with may come rushing into that formerly busy and crowded space. If you relax and allow yourself to courageously face what shows up, you'll start to disappear it.

Emptying yourself of "shoulds" and "in-order-tos" that run you without you being aware of it lets you ask better questions. You might see yourself as someone you don't truly know.

Be curious about what that person wants, needs, values, and cares about without the interference of outside influences or tons of mind clutter. That "stranger" you meet might have the inspiration, energy, and creativity to build you a very cool and bodaciously badass Sexy Second Act.

"N" Remodeling Techniques:

- Pick your favorite "N" word from this chapter as your theme for the day or week. Write it down and keep it with you.

- What resonates with you about this word? Journal your thoughts.

- Use your "N" word in conversation. Share with someone what it means to you. Ask what it means to them. Write down any insights that open up.

- Take at least one action consistent with the word you chose.

- Does an "N" word that's not on this list resonate with you? Write it down and do the exercises on this page with the word you chose.

- Choose a time period (one day, week, or month) and make your first answer "no" to everything anyone asks of you. If you cannot say "no" directly, say, "Let me think about it" or, "Let me get back to you."

- Notice your level of discomfort. Notice how you feel about the request. Is it something you want to do or something you feel obligated to do? How willing are you to say "yes" to only those things that you genuinely feel good about doing? Write down any epiphanies you have.

OBSERVER

A male acquaintance once shared something he did when his girlfriend broke up with him. He said that in the midst of his pain, he got the notion to look at himself in the mirror. He thought, "Oh, so that's what I look like when I cry. How interesting."

I was new to transformational work at the time, and I thought that was just plain weird. But my inner observer took note and tucked that tidbit away for future reference.

It popped back up when I went through a breakup. I made the mistake of watching a romantic movie. By the end of the movie I was crying and sinking deeply into feeling sorry for myself. I was lamenting the "fact" that no one loved me, never did, and never would.

As my despair deepened, my inner observer showed up and whispered clearly into my ear, "Aren't you the funny one? This is a really familiar place for you, isn't it? All this sadness, self-pity and drama!"

I stopped crying, shocked by this revelation. It was true. It was a familiar place and I realized how warm-and-fuzzy-comfortable it was. I even felt a little annoyed that by busting me, my inner "observer" had now made it impossible for me to go there.

I began to laugh at how funny and nuts it was to want to go to a painful place. We love the familiar, even when it hurts. Better the devil we know than the devil we don't know.

What once would have taken me days, months, or years to get over got handled in a few minutes. It was an epiphany. I saw that I no longer needed to go to that place. I could find better ways to give myself love, like calling a friend and getting together for bread pudding and whiskey sauce.

Of course, I still go dramatic and feel sorry for myself sometimes. But it's usually a drive-by these days. I don't move into the neighborhood.

Pay attention to your Inner Observer, Higher Self, God-voice, or whatever you choose to call that compassionate, truth-telling voice. It will help you see beyond the emotional experience you are having and will call your attention to your sometimes unworkable interpretation … or should I say misinterpretation … of events. The events of your life are real, but how you interpret them isn't.

In my case, my relationship had ended. That was real. My interpretation that I wasn't lovable and never would be was not real.

When you realize that your interpretations are just interpretations and not true, you can let go of believing them. When you let go of believing them, the door opens for you to create new interpretations that serve you.

I learned a lot about myself thanks to that relationship. Rather than feeling bitter and angry, or feeling sorry for myself, I am actually grateful to have had that experience. It made me better and stronger and more aware of what kind of relationship I want.

Meditation, exercise, and journaling are a few great practices to help you gain access to your inner observer. The more you practice, the easier it becomes to recognize and follow that inner voice that always has your back, wishes nothing but good for you, and knows exactly what you need in order to grow into exactly the person you are meant to become.

Give yourself the gift of getting acquainted with your inner observer. It's wonderful when there are people in your life who have your back. It's downright sexy when you have your own back.

ONE

"One" may not seem like a sexy or bodaciously badass word at first. You may think of "one" as the loneliest number. You may balk if someone declares you to be "the one," since it comes with high expectations you may not be ready or willing to live up to. Messy.

This is especially true when it comes to romance, especially if someone declares that you are the "one" who completes them. Until you don't. Because you can't. So the other person must leave you to find the "real one." Messy drama, chaos and pain.

Maybe you are someone who believes you are the only "one" you can rely on. No one does it better, faster, or more efficiently than you. You leave others feeling inadequate and disempowered.

As a result, you end up with a whole bunch of spinning plates to handle. You resent it and end up being a martyr. Others eventually give up or go away. Messy when plates get dropped. You are left alone with stress, drama, and pain.

Are you the "cool one?" Are you so cool you believe everyone everywhere should be at your immediate beck and call at all hours of the day and night? There's no room for anyone else to love you because you are so freaking in love with yourself. Messy. Someone is likely to come along and knock you off your pompous little pedestal.

Needless to say, these are less than stellar examples of what it means to be "the one." So what does a bodaciously badass "one" look like?

It's you—being the "one" for yourself—owning, accepting, and being 100% in charge of yourself. All of yourself, the good, the bad, and the ugly. You are "the one" who owns the circumstances of your life and how you manage them.

Notice I said "own" the circumstances, not "cause" the circumstances. You are not responsible for earthquakes, tsunamis, or the fact that your next door neighbor's bass keeps you awake every single night.

Own how you respond, not by finding fault, being a victim, or making

ONE

excuses, but by managing your responses with dignity, power, and compassion. You handle life exactly as it shows up without adding messy interpretations to it.

Acknowledge and have as much compassion for your own foibles as you do for anyone else's. Acknowledge your humanity and your imperfections without making excuses.

Set clear boundaries. Communicate what you want clearly and directly, with no hidden agenda.

Be wholesomely and awesomely curious and delighted with yourself and others. Cherish the gift of being alive. Concern yourself with serving others, and use your unique gifts to impact areas that matter to you.

"One" is a powerful number when you think about it like this:

- Changing your direction by only one degree will, over time, take you to a completely new destination.
- Replacing one unworkable habit with one good habit can dramatically change the direction of your health, finances, relationships, or career path.
- Replacing one limiting belief with one empowering belief can take you from victimhood to greater confidence and control.

It may not feel natural, at first, to be the "one" in that way. We are trained out of it at a young age. R. Buckminster Fuller says, "All children are born geniuses and we spend the first six years of their lives degeniusing them."

So be patient. Rediscovering your "genius" takes time and your willingness to do the work. The longer it's been since you were six, the deeper you may have to dig to find it.

Are you brave enough to dig through the muck of your limiting beliefs? Think of it as an excavation project, and you are the miner digging for gold.

What you'll discover about your true genius is priceless. Tapping into it is an important first step in turning your inner gold into outer riches. Be the "one" who uses your genius to design and build a rewarding, meaningful and fulfilling Sexy Second Act.

ORGASM

Never fear. This isn't going to be an anatomy lesson. There is more than enough information out there if you want help with that.

Anyway, why would you limit yourself to physical orgasms? There are other kinds that are awesomely cool, too, and they have a lot of similarities.

Let's talk about the similarities when it comes to setting goals. Reaching your goals requires effort. They don't just happen by themselves.

Just because it requires effort doesn't mean it can't be interesting, challenging, and fun. There's more than one way to get there. That's part of the fun. If you can't get there one way, try an alternate route.

If you focus on achieving an orgasm as the end result, you are liable to sabotage it and push it further away. That's also true of goals. It's OK to keep your eyes on the prize, but getting there will be a lot more fun if you focus on enjoying the moment.

The closer you get to the finish line of your goal, the greater the tension. But you can't hold that tension forever. If you stop or back off, you are left feeling frustrated and unfulfilled.

If you keep going until you reach your goal, the mounting tension eventually releases itself in a paroxysm of ecstasy. That fireworks moment of ecstasy when you reach your goal is your reward for a job well-done. This is the moment when you hear the theme from the 1976 movie, *Rocky*, playing in your head and you throw your arms up in a victory salute.

When it's all over, you get to relax and bask in the fulfilling afterglow of joy, love and accomplishment. Temporarily. Sooner or later, you'll get restless and want to do it all over again. You sexy devil, you.

Lots of yummy orgasms give you a juicy sex life. Lots of yummy goals give you a juicy, wildly orgasmic life experience. Who couldn't benefit from more of that in their Second Act?

Bet you never thought of achieving a goal as an orgasmic experience. Knowing that now, what difference will it make in how you set goals from here on out?

"O" Remodeling Techniques:

- Pick an "O" word from this chapter as your theme for the day or week. Write it down and keep it with you.

- What resonates with you about this word? Journal or meditate on your thoughts.

- Use your "O" word in conversation. Share what it means to you with someone. Ask what it means to them. Write down any insights that open up.

- Take at least one action consistent with the word you chose.

- Does a different "O" word resonate with you? Write it down and do the exercises on this page with the word you chose.

- Spend a few minutes every day "observing" your reactions. Do you notice patterns about what triggers you? What "one" change can you make to gain freedom in that area? Make the change and write down your insights.

P

PASSION

For a number of years, I had the honor and privilege of coaching a course whose goal was to train and develop participants to express themselves freely and powerfully. The path to that goal was to create a project and complete it during the program.

The purpose of the project was to help participants recognize where they were blocking their self-expression, so they could receive training in how to demolish them. The coaches helped by assisting participants to design projects that met the course criteria and to keep the participants in action on their projects through the duration of the course.

Creating my own projects and helping participants create theirs taught me a lot. I learned that passion and purpose are compelling ingredients for designing successful projects and lives.

I learned that behind every successful project was something that mattered to the participant. When participants combined what mattered to them with something they loved, seemingly impossible projects came together in miraculous ways.

One of my favorite projects was launched by Al Nomura, owner of Al Nomura Photography in Orange County, California. Al is a wonderful photographer who has a heart for kids. He created a project using photography (what he loves) to make a difference for kids with cancer (where he wanted to make a difference).

He gathered a group of volunteer photographers together and paired them with kids undergoing cancer treatment. The photographers spent a day with the kids, helping them take pictures of things they love. He named his project "Things That Make My Face Say Cheese."

It was a beautiful and inspiring project. People couldn't wait to jump on board and assist. Volunteers printed and framed the photos. A gallery owner put them on display and catered a showing. Another volunteer trademarked the name.

The project was so successful Al was invited to display the kids' photos and the video he created at the Orange County Fair here in Southern California. His "paycheck" was the knowledge that his project touched many people: the kids, their families, the volunteer photographers, and everyone who saw the exhibit at the OC Fair. He was paid in tangible ways, too, with new business opportunities from people who were inspired by his project.

If you feel stuck in figuring out how to design your Sexy Second Act, start with what you love. Add what you care about. Don't worry about a paycheck just yet. When you get your passion and purpose sorted out, you'll be able to strategize ways to get paid. In the beginning, let yourself dream!

If turning your world upside down is too scary, or you aren't in a position to do that just now, start small with one project. Share your idea with people you trust and be open to seeing where your project goes.

At worst, you will meet new people to network with. At best, your project may take on a life of its own as other people become inspired. Many projects become the foundation for starting a new career, launching a business, or starting a nonprofit organization.

The key is to begin, even if you don't know how it will turn out. You are doing your project as an expression of what you love and what matters to you. Sharing your passion for your project will inspire others. Stick with it and before you know it, you may just find yourself off and running on your Sexy Second Act.

PLAY

The "Things That Make My Face Say Cheese" project was all about play. The kids were so happy and excited. They couldn't wait to take pictures of things they loved and share them with their families and friends.

They weren't worried about composition or lighting or what anyone else thought about what they photographed. They ran around having fun with their cameras and their new photographer friends. Focusing on having fun and sharing things that made them smile, helped them temporarily forget about the difficulty of what they were going through.

A day where they could escape the stress of dealing with their disease may have even helped their healing. Instead of focusing on their treatment, they now had a happy memory to focus on.

My friend Teri once invited me to help her lead a session where participants were asked to put their attention on play and what they love. An older lady attending the session had a number of physical ailments. She saw life as hard and boring. She believed she had "done it all" and that, in her mid-seventies, there was nothing left. In a sense, she was waiting to die.

The transformation was dramatic when she let that go and played at putting her attention on what she loved; activities like dancing and specific places she wanted to go.

She sat up straighter. Her eyes began to sparkle. Her skin color brightened. Much of the pain left her body. She looked at least twenty years younger.

Her brain was stubborn and kept returning her focus to life being hard, boring, and over. Every time she shifted her focus, she aged. The sparkle left her eyes and she looked pale and wan.

That was powerful for everyone in the session to see. The same thing happened to everyone who participated in the exercise, but the difference showed up most dramatically in this woman. It became abundantly evident that all work and no play really does make Jacks—and Jills—dull boys and girls.

You might think it's hard to put play into your life on a daily basis, but it's not as hard as you think. The question is—are you willing to let your inner child out?

I once worked on a particularly stressful project where a coworker kept fun things on her desk, like Play-Doh and bubble blowing solution. Someone would start playing during a break and soon others would join in. There was always laughter around her desk. After the play break, everyone returned to their tasks feeling refreshed, energized, and with a bounce in their steps.

Make play a priority. Make time to laugh. Make time to do things you love with people who enjoy playing. Don't put play off for retirement. You may not live that long if you don't make time for play!

Take vacations. Schedule play dates and play weekends into your calendar the same way you schedule anything else.

I once coached a woman who ran her own health and fitness business. She was concerned because she and her husband were working so hard, they barely saw each other. When they did, they were too exhausted to make time for themselves as a married couple. She felt like they were drifting apart.

I asked her what she thought might work to bring them closer. She wanted to have at least one weekend off a month and one week off every three months. But she felt like it was impossible with a business to run.

I asked her to have a conversation with her husband and ask for his support to help her make it happen. They got out their calendar and scheduled those weekends and weeks off for the entire year. By doing that, they could arrange for their jobs to be covered well in advance.

It's interesting what happens when you make taking care of yourself a priority. She came back from her first weekend away with her hubby smiling and looking refreshed with a jaunty bounce in her step.

Make time for play and you'll live longer and healthier. You'll attract a passel of new friends, because people love to be around playful people who enjoy life. Playful people are sexy!

PURPOSE

I don't know of anyone who wants to feel useless. Feeling like you don't matter is the start of all sorts of mischief. People who don't feel important in a healthy and positive way will find a not-so-appealing way to feel significant. Terrorism is an extreme example of that.

Thinking you don't matter is one more useless dictate emanating from the committee in your head. Please stop listening to it. It's bunk!

If you want to feel important, make others feel important. If play is missing from your life, help others to play. If you want love in your life, love others.

Create a purpose that makes a difference for others and you will never feel useless or insignificant again. It doesn't have to be hard, heavy, or serious! That nonsense has gotten our world into the yucky muck it's in. We need to design a lighthearted and edgy purpose that matters to us, like these examples from clients:

- to see the value and uniqueness of every person
- to soar through life with courage
- to shake things up and rabble-rouse
- to put kindness where it's needed
- to have the balls to play big
- to tell the truth and kick butt
- to let my little kid out

Do you think these funny, edgy, simple purpose statements (or mission statements, if you like) can be life-changers and difference-makers? I sure do!

The interesting part is that when each of these clients got clear about what their purpose was, it showed up like something they knew but hadn't seen clearly; like an "of course." I have also seen them moved to tears when they recognize, for the very first time, what they are here to do.

One of my favorites comes from a drummer friend who has known he was meant to be a drummer since he was three. Part of his purpose is to "tune in to the rhythm of the Universe." Of course it is.

PURPOSE

Not everyone is clear about their purpose from the age of three. You may need more life experience to get a sense of who you are and what you came here to do.

I didn't discover mine—to passionately, powerfully, and playfully celebrate life—until after I left my corporate job. It took a ton of soul-searching for me to uncover it. It's also undergone a few iterations since I first got the sense of it.

There's no right or wrong timing. However and whenever you get it is excellent. You only need to be willing to believe a couple of things:

- You came here to be of service, either directly or by example.
- Your service will make a difference for others and fulfill you.

You may be living your purpose already, without consciously realizing it. One way to start distinguishing it is to ask trusted friends and colleagues to describe you in one or two words or a phrase. You may recognize a pattern or theme that forms the roots of your Purpose.

Once you distinguish it, you'll start to see the world through that lens. You'll see how you can apply it to your Sexy Second Act career, business, relationships, health, finances, and spiritual practices.

You will feel the chaos of your world start to organize itself in a brand-new, beautiful, and sexy way. You will magnetize new opportunities to you that allow you to express your purpose.

The world needs what you came here to do. What it doesn't need is for you to suppress who you are or sacrifice your joy to do it. This is no time to mess around with nonsense like that. Pick a project, add your passion and purpose, and get a move on. It's time to get "sexy!"

"P" Remodeling Techniques:

- Pick a "P" word from this chapter as your theme for the day or week. Write it down and keep it with you.

- What resonates with you about this word? Journal or meditate your thoughts.

- Use your "P" word in conversation. Share what it means to you with someone. Ask what it means to them. Write down any insights that open up.

- Take at least one action consistent with the word you chose.

- Does a different "P" word resonate with you? Write it down and do the exercises on this page with the word you chose.

- Set a weekly play date with a friend or loved one. Keep the date and don't let anything come up that would allow you to cancel it. Do things you wouldn't normally do. Go to an art museum. Take a golf lesson together. Stay overnight in a resort hotel. Get a couples' massage. Eat at an ethnic restaurant. Wear offbeat clothes.

- Make a list of things you love and of those who might benefit from a project you create for them. Example: Love sports and have a passion for kids with disabilities? Play with ideas for a project to take them to a sports event. Share with friends and colleagues willing to brainstorm ways to make it happen.

QUALITY QUESTIONS

Aside from running your bodily functions, your brain is designed to solve problems. You have a choice about what kinds of problems you give it.

If you ask questions about why you are stupid, unattractive, not good enough, unlovable, or insignificant, your brain will give you a gazillion answers. But how will that make a difference in your life, other than to confirm your limiting beliefs?

Ask bodaciously badass questions instead. Ask questions that uplift and inspire you and help you create a quality life. Ask questions like these:

- What is my life about?
- What matters to me?
- What makes me happy?
- Where can I contribute my skills in a positive and powerful way that's fun, fulfilling and makes a difference?
- With whom do I want to spend quality time?
- What am I grateful for?
- What lessons can I learn from the challenges in my life?
- What would I like to master or accomplish?
- What legacy do I want to leave?

Stay away from "why" questions. They put the committee in your head on alert to get defensive and cranky. Or it will tell you lies. Think back to when your mom asked why you never clean up your room. There's nothing like a "why" question to make you feel made wrong, small, and un-sexy.

"How" questions won't get you very far, either. "How" questions, especially if you are doing something you've never done before, are likely to stop you in your tracks. Play with "what, where, when, and who" questions. The answers to those questions will help you figure out the "how."

Asking quality questions forces you to give up "knowing." If you don't think so, try this experiment. Next time you are with someone you think you

QUALITY QUESTIONS

know well, ask them to tell you two things about themselves you don't already know. And be ready to share two things they don't know about you. Don't be surprised if the quality of your entire conversation shifts dramatically and becomes more interesting, lively, and fun. That's the power of quality questions.

Don't let yourself get away with "knowing" you can't create something bodaciously badass cool as you delve into creating your Sexy Second Act. There's always something you don't know, the discovery of which can dramatically alter the course of your life!

Quality questions wake up the whispers of curiosity. Curiosity is sexy. It opens up the possibility of learning something new, seeing life differently, or at least making for lively and interesting conversations.

At the very least, you'll get a little bit smarter. Being smart is totally sexy!

QUIET

I used to have a mind that raced like the wind … a catastrophic whirlwind! It swirled and twirled and raged across the landscape of my life, telling me how scary it was "out there." I worried about everything and tried to outguess all possible scenarios that might occur with people, places, and things. It was my attempt to keep my world "safe."

Do you know how exhausting that is? Anxiety took a physical and emotional toll on my life for a long time.

Quiet moments were few and far between and happened mostly when I was on a camping vacation somewhere in nature. Only then was I able to be somewhat present and quiet.

My mind still races. That blasted committee never shuts up. But it feels less like a whirlwind these days. I'm learning to slow it down and redirect the committee's attention toward giving me productive and positive feedback!

Personally, I don't like traditional meditation. I admire you if you are someone who can get into it.

Luckily, if you are like me, there are a variety of helpful practices available for quieting your committee's ruckus. Exercise. Walks outside. Breathing. Asking quality questions. Consciously noticing what your body is doing, such as feeling your feet as they take each step, eating slowly and savoring each bite, or picking something to look at in great detail, like a painting or a rose.

One of my favorites is to conduct a body scan. Pay attention to your toes and appreciate the job they do of keeping you balanced when you walk. Appreciate your feet for connecting you to the earth and for carrying you around. Appreciate your ankles, calves, knees and so forth until you have acknowledged and expressed gratitude for every part of your body, inside and out.

This practice can help you fall asleep when the committee wants to focus on the events of your day or tomorrow's problems. You may never get all the way to your head before you fall asleep. That's great! Start at your head and go the other way next time.

Experiment to find practices that work for you. If you persist, you'll find ones that work to help you achieve a delicious break from thinking.

You are fully in Act II when your committee is quiet. In Act II, you can appreciate that you are part of all things—a miracle in a Universe of miracles. That's a sexy space!

QUIT

Knowing when and what to quit is totally sexy. If you have even one teeny thought that you are overwhelmed or overcommitted, it's OK to become a quitter.

Quit giving your time and energy to every demand that shows up knocking at your front door. Quit trying to be all things to all people.

Quit being busy for the sake of being busy.

Quit giving your power away. Quit being a victim. Quit dancing to someone else's tune.

Quit taking care of others without taking care of yourself. Quit letting others step over your boundaries.

Quit putting off what's important to you. Quit thinking that you have little or nothing to contribute.

Quit being a Negative Nelly or Ned. Quit gossiping. Quit judging.

Quit believing what anyone else thinks. Quit believing what you think.

Quit arguing about the same old thing. Quit the drama. Quit stinkin' thinkin'.

Quit hoping. It's not a strategy.

Quit comparing yourself and your journey to anyone else's. Their path is their path and yours is yours.

Quit worrying about things outside your control. Quit thinking you can fix anyone.

Quit it. Just quit it. Quit anything or anyone that drains you in body, mind, heart, or spirit.

Start doing things and being with people who energize and enliven you. You'll live longer and healthier, and you'll be happier.

Quitting what drains you and starting what energizes you is sexy! Choose the sexy path!

"Q" Remodeling Techniques:

- Pick a "Q" word from this chapter as your theme for the day or week. Write it down and keep it with you.

- What resonates with you about this word? Journal or meditate your thoughts.

- Use your "Q" word in conversation. Share what it means to you with someone. Ask what it means to them. Write down any insights that open up.

- Take at least one action consistent with the word you chose.

- Does a different "Q" word resonate with you? Write it down and do the exercises on this page with the word you chose.

- Answer the Quality Question from this chapter. Add your own what, where, who, and when questions. Stay away from "why" or "how" questions. "Why" questions make you go into your head for an answer. "How" questions will keep you from moving forward. You'll figure out the "how" as you go along.

R

RENEGADE

A renegade is generally considered to be someone who rejects one religion, cause, or allegiance, and who turns to another. That's not generally perceived as a good thing.

But there are times when going renegade is not only appropriate, it's mandatory. It's sexy to take a walk on the wild side from time to time.

Renegades change the world. How about the Wright brothers, Steve Jobs, Picasso, the suffragettes, Madonna, Amelia Earhart, and your favorite superhero?

Renegades don't let themselves be put into boxes. They never use phrases like, "That's just how I am; how life is; how they are; how 'it' is."

Renegades don't limit themselves. They are willing to let go of certainty and look at themselves, their lives, them, and "it" and create something different.

I used to get a new-age catalog. One issue featured a weeklong trip to Sedona, Arizona. I wanted badly to go, but I balked at signing up because I didn't have anyone to go with. I'd never been on vacation by myself, and the prospect of going alone felt daunting. I didn't know myself as someone who vacationed alone.

The committee in my head started up about how I wouldn't have a good time by myself; how everyone else would have company and wouldn't talk to me; and how it would be a waste of money to go and be miserable. Yada-yada.

But, my renegade self wasn't having the committee's nonsense. I thought about that trip for days. I picked up that catalog so often, it automatically fell open to the page describing the trip. My renegade self knew I'd regret it forever if I didn't go. I picked up the phone and bought myself a ticket.

Needless to say, it turned out to be one of my favorite vacations. I met fabulous people. Every day was a wonderful adventure of sightseeing and spiritual practices.

The best part was learning I could go on vacation by myself and have a great time. If that's not a confidence builder, then what is? Confidence is sexy!

Letting my inner renegade out taught me to follow my intuition. I'm learning to pay attention when she gets restless. My inner renegade never steers me wrong.

I believe people come to coaching when they want to let their inner renegades out. They want permission to trade in what they "should" or "shouldn't" do for what they want to do.

I recently got a call from an acquaintance who felt something was off in her current job. She has lots of responsibility and makes good money, but it isn't really what she wants. When I asked her to describe what she'd like to do, she knew exactly what it was, but she couldn't quite bring herself to take a leap of faith and go for it.

We talked about what it would take for her to feel good about jumping. It came down to making a plan for how much money she'd need to support her during the gap while she developed her business.

It was fun to watch her demeanor change to excitement and anticipation when she realized her dream was doable. She can enjoy the job she's got knowing that it's a bridge job that will take her to her dream job.

Renegades have fun. Renegades color outside the lines. Renegades have big, juicy dreams that make a difference. Renegades dance on the edge.

Renegades are willing to explore unknown territory. They hear a different tune and follow a different drummer. Think Cleopatra or Braveheart (Sir William Wallace), or Muhammad Ali.

What would your inner renegade love you to do? What would it take for you to do it and live the Sexy Second Act life you dream of living?

RESPONSIBILITY

Coming from a childhood where I wasn't taught much about responsibility, learning to accept it as an adult was challenging. I had a lot of growing up to do once I went out on my own.

I was a grown-up about handling financial responsibility. I got a job, moved into an apartment, paid my bills on time, and never asked my parents or anyone else for financial support. Money was often tight, but I made it work.

But for many years, I didn't take responsibility for how other parts of my life went. When things didn't turn out, it was someone else's fault, the economy's fault, my boss's fault, how I was raised … or, well … you get the picture.

Underneath blaming, of course, I had a myriad of limiting beliefs about my ability to take responsibility for myself. Limiting beliefs form a shaky foundation for building a strong house. I constantly worried that my house would come tumbling down. When would I get fired? When would my relationship go south? When would "they" find out I'm a fraud?

Before I could build my Sexy Second Act, I had to demolish my limiting belief that I had little or no control over my life. I had to learn how to give up being a victim. I had to stop letting myself off the hook for how my life was going.

I thought it was ridiculous when I first heard that I am responsible for everything that happens in my life. The committee jumped on that idea like ducks on a June bug. Earthquakes, terrorism, swings in the economy. Really? You've gotta be kidding!

No, you can't control everything. What you can control is how you respond to everything, even earthquakes, terrorism, and swings in the economy. You can start by asking quality questions like these:

- What is the best and most empowering way to respond to what's happening?

RESPONSIBILITY

- What would be the best outcome?
- What steps can I take to resolve this problem or situation?

Relationships are a great training ground for learning to take responsibility, especially during arguments. Calling the person you love a jerk in the midst of an argument is not the most empowering response. It won't give you the outcome you want or lead to a good resolution.

Arguments often disguise underlying concerns having nothing to do with the argument. Taking a moment to calm down and step back until you can figure out the underlying concern and deal with it, regardless of who started the argument, is an example of taking responsibility.

Oftentimes, you can nip negative outcomes in the bud by taking responsibility. You can turn an argument into a problem-solving discussion.

Taking responsibility doesn't mean it will always turn out the way you want. You may have to take responsibility for knowing when it's time to let go.

My friend Kim has the perfect motto for accepting responsibility. She says that no matter how something turns out, it's perfect. Why? Because that's how it turned out.

That might sound like giving up and being resigned but it's not. Responsibility is giving 100% of yourself to every situation. If you can look at yourself in the mirror, knowing you are doing your very best, you can let go of how it turns out. If it goes well, love and be grateful for your results. If it doesn't turn out like you wanted it to, learn and be grateful for the lesson.

It's a win for you either way. You'll enjoy celebrating your victories and you'll move through the pain of your losses without suffering.

RIGOR

A friend of mine called himself a "Procrastinator Extraordinaire" in response to an article he shared on Facebook. I had to smile because that's me. Growing up, I never learned to be rigorous with myself about anything.

During my training as a coach, I had to deal with my own resistance. My coaches often reminded me to be rigorous with my intentions, my thinking, and my actions.

Ugh! Like it or not, I had to confront the reasons I consistently fell short of completing things. I squirmed. I avoided. I shut down. Resistance had me by the throat.

My coaches were rigorous and refused to let me off the hook. I didn't make it easy on them or myself. My pattern was to covertly resist. I made promises week after week and failed to live up to them.

My coaches stood firm. They consistently held me to account for generating breakthroughs that would lift up my life game to the level I wanted to play.

"What does procrastinating cost you?" they asked me. I resisted looking. I didn't want to see that part of myself. The cost was lost dreams, stress, depression, sadness, and loneliness.

"What's the payoff?" they asked me. That was no fun to look at, either. The payoff was that I could hide out and avoid being criticized for not doing something correctly. I could avoid being "controlled" by others. I could avoid failing. I could avoid humiliation.

The paradox was that by procrastinating, I failed anyway and experienced the humiliation I wanted to avoid. Not pretty.

As Gloria Steinem once famously said, "The truth will set you free. But first it will piss you off."

I read somewhere that discipline is about remembering what you love. If that's the case, then rigor is about staying true to what you love.

Everyone gets sidetracked in life. Forget about judging yourself for going off course. You're human; it happens. Rigorously ask yourself quality questions, tell yourself the truth, confront obstacles, and do what it takes to overcome them. You are in training for your version of the Olympics. Want the medal? Be rigorous!

Long-lasting buildings have a strong structure. Rigor includes building yourself a support structure to keep you on course until you succeed. Every champion has a coach or mentor committed to helping him or her win. Top-performing business people belong to mastermind groups and have boards of directors.

Strong people develop rigorous practices. They use tools like vision boards, mantras, and journaling to help them stay the course until they reach their dreams.

Rigor is focus—on steroids. It's where the rubber meets the road. Rigor means taking the next step when you don't feel like it. Rigor leads to mastery. Rigor writes books, runs marathons, raises families, and builds sustainable careers, relationships, and businesses. Rigor keeps you tuned in to your truest self and intentions.

Rigor puts you on the road to gold. Winning the gold is deliciously sexy!

"R" Remodeling Techniques:

- Pick an "R" word from this chapter as your theme for the day or week. Write it down and keep it with you.

- What resonates with you about this word? Journal or meditate your thoughts.

- Use your "R" word in conversation. Share what it means to you with someone. Ask what it means to them. Write down any insights that open up.

- Take at least one action consistent with the word you chose.

- Does a different "R" word resonate with you? Write it down and do the exercises on this page with the word you chose.

- Who is your favorite renegade? It can be someone living or dead, or a comic superhero like Superman or Wonder Woman. Write down who it is. Next time you face a problem or dilemma, ask yourself what your favorite renegade would do in this situation. Stand like they would stand. Talk as they would talk. Move like they would move. Did you come up with some interesting ideas? Take action on them.

S

SERENDIPITY

Some words are just plain fun to say. "Serendipity" is one such word. You've likely read it often enough throughout this book. How could it not be included as a word?

I think of serendipity as God's way of being playful with us, delighting us, and surprising us. To me, it represents God's way of letting us know we've been heard, we're on the right track, and it's our reward for being rigorously true to ourselves.

I never did have much use for a God who punishes us. I think we do enough of that ourselves. I can believe all day—and twice on Sunday—in a God who loves us and wants us to be happy. Perhaps serendipity is God's signal that we are on the right track.

The 2004 movie *What the Bleep Do We Know?* awakened me to the power of awareness and the power of aligning our heart, mind, and spirit with our highest intentions. What brought it home was this quote by Dr. Joe Dispenza from the movie:

"I wake up in the morning and I consciously create my day the way I want it to happen ... But here's the thing: When I create my day and out of nowhere little things happen that are so unexplainable, I know that they are the process or the result of my creation. And the more I do that, the more I build a neural net in my brain that I accept that that's possible. (This) gives me the power and the incentive to do it the next day...

"... 'Now if (it) is in fact the observer's watching me the whole time that I'm doing this and there is a spiritual aspect to myself, then show me a sign today that you paid attention to any one of these things that I created, and bring them in a way that I won't expect, so I'm as surprised at my ability to be able to experience these things. And make it so that I have no doubt that it's come from you,' and so I live my life, in a sense, all day long thinking about being a genius or thinking about being the glory and the power of God or thinking about being unconditional love."

Serendipity is a reminder that every single thought you think is a prayer, not just the conscious thoughts you think in church or when you are down on our knees. Like it or not, whether you are consciously creating or unconsciously creating, you are responsible for the life you are building.

You can remodel your thinking by consciously creating your day. Give serendipity the opportunity to show up to play. It takes practice, and you may not see results right away.

But don't worry. Serendipity isn't going anywhere. She's standing by, ready to help you amp up your "sexy" factor in fun and delightful ways that are even better than you anticipate.

SEXY

Sexy sells for a reason. Everyone wants to be sexy. Or feel sexy. When it's authentic, it's juicy!

The kind of sexy I'm talking about isn't what you might think of as romantic. Romantic sexy is often about the tease, like Lucy in the Charles Schultz *Peanuts* comic strip that began in 1950 and still runs in syndication. She promises poor Charlie Brown she won't pull the football away. And poor sucker Charlie falls for it. Every. Single. Time. The tease is the promise of something that's never going to be delivered. But the tease keeps you hoping.

Advertising is often about just such a tease, promising you the sexy gal or guy if you buy the car, cologne, or toothpaste. Abusers understand the tease, promising to change their ways if you give them one more chance. Once they have you "hooked," they revert to their abusive behavior.

Authentic sexy is very different. It includes a heart-to-heart connection and mutual respect. There's a mutual consent to being playful and flirty. There's aliveness and vitality to it. There's love in it. Best of all, there's creation in it.

It's awesome to have a partner, but it's not necessary. You can be bodaciously badass sexy without one by connecting to your own heart and committing yourself to flirting and playing with your biggest and juiciest dreams. What better way to create an orgasmic experience of living than being madly besotted with yourself and the life you are creating?

There's nothing better for making things joyfully go your way than being turned on by who you are and what you are doing. When you get turned on by your own "life game," you become a magnet for attracting what you dream of and want. You will soon have playful partners leaping out of the woodwork to cavort on your juicy, sexy playground with you!

Happy is sexy. Laughing is sexy. Doing what you love—and doing it your way—is sexy. Doing what you love in service to others is sexy.

Being turned on by your life generates heat—a synergy of ideas, creativity and curiosity. Sexy life games kill off resignation, depression, and boredom.

Turned-on people get lucky. They move in a giddy-asmic bubble, living a juicy life filled with amazing people. They give birth to cool projects, jobs, businesses, and relationships.

Sexy is being your true, authentic self without apology. Sexy is standing up for what you believe. Sexy is being clear about what you want and asking for it directly and without manipulation. Sexy is having gratitude for what you have.

One way to start is to think about who your heroes are. What are the qualities about them that attract you?

You have those qualities within you or you wouldn't recognize or resonate with them in your heroes. What actions can you cultivate and model from their actions to design and build your Sexy Second Act?

SO WHAT?

A friend of mine has a roller coaster relationship with money. When she's making money, she's happy and in her groove.

When the pipeline slows down, she panics, goes into a depression and stops doing anything productive for her business. She gets "busy" doing whatever she can to distract herself. When high demands are placed on her, what she hears in her head is, "I don't want to, I don't want to, I don't want to!"

Another client procrastinates when she gets scared by what she thinks she can't do or if she thinks she'll fail. When it becomes more painful or stressful to avoid the situation than to take action, she will finally do what she needs to do to meet the deadline or get it done. She's usually left wondering why she allowed herself to suffer for so long.

Still another client wants to get married and have a family. He has a myriad of "reasons" why this is never going to happen for him. His reasons keep him from putting himself out there to meet women who might be terrific candidates for a committed relationship.

Reasons. Excuses. Fear. Avoidance. Distraction. These are dream killers.

Not long ago I heard someone say that on the other side of what's so is … so what? Consider:

- You are afraid … so what?
- You don't want to … so what?
- You have reasons and excuses … so what?

One way to stop the committee in its tracks is to ask yourself, "So what?" It interrupts your thinking long enough for you to ask yourself, "Huh? What do you mean, 'so what?'"

That's when you have an opportunity to get genuinely curious and ask yourself quality questions about what you are committed to. Questions such as:

- Are you committed to being afraid or are you committed to having your dream?

SO WHAT?

- Are you committed to struggling to survive or are you committed to living abundantly?
- Are you committed to your reasons or are you committed to creating a juicy, sexy, fulfilling life that matters?

So what? So what? Do you want to stay locked in the prison of your past, or would you rather be a renegade pioneer on the journey to designing and building a sexy, purposeful, and passionate Second Act? You are the "one" who gets to take responsibility and choose.

SURRENDER

Have I mentioned that I love epiphanies? One of mine came from a seminar leader who said that being "stuck" is about being stubborn. OMG, did that hit a nerve!

We don't get stuck; we stick ourselves. There's no glue pinning us to the floor. The committee in our head sticks us to our fear when we believe the reasons it gives us for why we can't move forward. As an acquaintance of mine often says, "Can't resides on Won't Street."

Yep. Sure does.

Surrender sounds so simple. And it is. That doesn't make it easy.

I'm not talking about the giving-up kind of surrender, nor the trudging-along-day-to-day-survival kind of resignation. That's low energy.

High energy surrender is yielding to possibility. Releasing what you think you know. Dancing in the unknown with curiosity, wonder, delight, playfulness, and an open heart.

Surrender isn't about giving up. Surrender is about letting go.

One night, many years ago, I crawled dejectedly into bed thinking that if I didn't wake up in the morning, it would be OK with me. I wasn't happy and I was tired of pretending to be happy. I'd reached the end of my rope and I didn't care much about hanging on.

It seems a little crazy looking back, because my life was pretty good. I had a good job that paid me well, great friends, and a nice little condo in a Southern California town where many people would love to live.

I had reached a low point and I knew something had to change. I didn't know exactly what, I just remember saying—or praying—that if things were to change, I needed help. Obviously, doing things my same old stubborn way wasn't working.

Some people say that when they surrendered to their Higher Power, God, or the Universe, they woke up to a different world. That was not my experience, although I think it would be way cool if it happened like that.

It's only now, looking back, that I can see how that night was a turning point. When I finally let go of being stubborn and I surrendered, Serendipity sauntered into my life.

Or maybe she was standing by and whispering in my ear all along. I just couldn't hear her.

Not long after that night, a coworker invited me to participate in a program that turned my entire belief system upside down. Thanks to that program, I learned how to "unstick" myself and let go of being stubborn.

I met people who were living lives I imagined were out of my reach. I made friends who taught me how to dream again and who supported and encouraged me to go for those dreams. It was the first step toward building my own Sexy Second Act.

By surrendering, you are actually taking responsibility for becoming the master builder of your life. You "unstick" yourself from being a victim, from blaming, from helplessness.

Surrender is tricky, though. You don't learn it just once. Or maybe I'm extra hard-headed and stubborn. My experience is that you have to learn it all over again every time you come up against something that scares the hell out of you or falls outside your comfort zone.

That's good to keep in mind so you don't beat yourself up when you realize you've stuck yourself ... again. You must constantly be on the lookout for what you are resisting and figure out what you need to let go of on the path to achieving the big, juicy goals you want.

You have to love the paradox—that surrendering gives you back your power. So simple. So challenging.

If it was easy, anybody could do it. But you aren't "anybody." You're "somebody." You matter. Your dreams matter.

Let go of the reasons and excuses for why you "can't." Move off of "Won't Street" and move onto "Pursuing Your Passion" Boulevard. Surrender to pursuing your dreams—with energy, vitality, and gusto!

"S" Remodeling Techniques:

- Pick an "S" word from this chapter as your theme for the day or week. Write it down and keep it with you.

- What resonates with you about this word? Journal or meditate your thoughts.

- Use your "S" word in conversation. Share what it means to you with someone. Ask what it means to them. Write down any insights that open up.

- Take at least one action consistent with the word you chose.

- Does a different "S" word resonate with you? Write it down and do the exercises on this page with the word you chose.

- The next time you feel stuck about something, see if you can identify what's behind your inability to move forward. Ask yourself, "So what?" As in … "I might fail … so what?" Then answer the question. Keep asking the question for every objection your "committee" comes up with until you find the freedom to move forward.

- Practice intentionally creating your day. The best time to do this is as soon as possible after you wake up. At the end of the day, do a quick review. Can you spot any instances of where Serendipity sauntered in to assist?

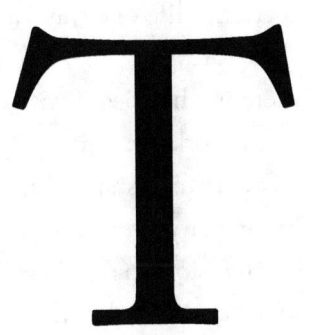

TRANSITION

There's no doubt about it. Transitions are unsettling. They're uncertain. You don't know what's going to happen, and you don't know how it's going to turn out.

Some transitions begin with events outside your control. You might be laid off, lose your home to a fire or flood, or lose someone you love. You might experience a natural disaster like an earthquake or you might experience a sudden economic crisis. You might find out your spouse wants a divorce or you might get a scary medical diagnosis.

Before the event, you experience life one way. In an instant, you recognize that life as you knew it, is gone forever.

Inside transitions are different. They begin with a "knowing" that it's time to leave a relationship that isn't working; quit a job you've outgrown; or end a friendship that's turned toxic. It may start with a faint sense of unease or restlessness that increases in intensity over time.

This kind of transition is often slow to manifest. You may not recognize it right away, and you may not act on it for months or years.

Inside transitions are easy to ignore at first. But the longer you ignore them, the unhappier or more stressed your life becomes. The sooner you pay attention, the greater your ability to process them and design an effective plan for going forward.

Be aware that your inside transition might trigger someone else's outside transition, like when you announce to your spouse that you want to go back to school, live in a foreign country, or start a business. Someone else's outside transition may trigger your internal transition. Consider:

- How will you deal with your kids going off to college and turning you into an empty-nester?
- How will your life change when your spouse loses his or her job?
- How will you manage a parent's loss of independence when they have to rely on you for support?

TRANSITION

A former client experienced an inside transition when it came to his relationship. He'd come close to proposing several times, but each time, something happened that caused him to back off.

He grappled with what to do for months. He swung back and forth between wanting to break up and believing that if he did, he would be "wasting" all the years he had invested in the relationship.

His struggle continued until a couple of events occurred that were game breakers for him. These events finally convinced him of what he already knew deep inside. It was time to end the relationship.

The breakup came as a shock to his girlfriend, who hadn't paid attention to red flags he'd been hoisting for months. His decision to end the relationship caused her world to come tumbling down. His inside transition became her outside transition.

My client eventually met and married the woman of his dreams. He left his job, started a business and is now raising a family. He is happy and doing well in his new life.

Looking back, I'm sure he's glad he trusted the inner wisdom that kept telling him his former relationship was not the right one for him. Once he surrendered to that wisdom, Serendipity stepped in to support his dream of finding an excellent relationship.

Societies undergo transitions as well. Here are just a few of the major events we've experienced over the last fifty or sixty years. They continue to impact how we see ourselves, each other, and our place in the world:

- We launched satellites into space, landed men on the moon, and traversed our entire solar system.
- Computers evolved from being an intimidating roomful of humming boxes, designed only for problem-solving, to connecting us to the entire world from a handheld device. Computers have eliminated borders. Technology is designing robots that do work once done manually.
- The Women's Movement, Civil Rights Movement, and Gay Rights

Movement altered our personal lives and the way we work.
- Medical science has evolved to the point where both the exact beginning and end of life are no longer as clear to us as they once seemed.
- The systems we depended on to "take care of us" are disintegrating one by one. Lifetime jobs are a thing of the past. Retirement as we've known it is well on the way to becoming extinct.

As a society, we are still reeling from the impact of these transitions. We resist and try to put things back the way we think they are "supposed" to be. And because these events are coming at us faster and faster, processing them becomes a huge challenge. We feel stressed and hard-pressed to cope.

Resistance keeps you focused on Act I. Focusing on the past makes it impossible to look forward. You can "stick yourself" to Act I, or you can choose to believe that what you gain from surrendering to events exactly as they are will make you stronger, lead you to a better life, or show you how you can best serve others in a way that excites, delights, and fulfills you.

You can go through a transition with grace by remembering that you are always in Act II. Let go of Act I. It's over and done. Embrace the present moment.

Choose to accept that your transition is preparing you for something new. Take the lesson and see how you can use it to create something powerful, fun, and sexy.

TRUST

Here comes another epiphany. You can trust anyone. You can count on them to be exactly the way they are and exactly the way they are not. Trust is only broken when you expect them to be any other way than the way they are.

You can trust a thief to be a thief, a liar to be a liar, and an unreliable person to be unreliable. You can trust an honorable person to be honorable, a loving person to be loving, and a spiritual person to be spiritual.

Expecting them to operate any other way than how they operate opens you up to being hurt, betrayed, and disappointed. Insanity is marrying an addict and expecting them to change or that you can change them. Insanity is expecting a gossip to keep your secrets. Insanity is expecting someone who constantly breaks promises to keep the ones made to you.

The problem for you isn't that the other person operates as an addict, gossip, or promise-breaker. That's their circumstance to deal with. The problem lies in your unwillingness to accept them exactly that way and take care of yourself accordingly.

That doesn't mean you give up on them or allow them to get away with unworkable behavior. You don't. Integrity is holding them accountable for the impact their behavior has on you. Integrity is also holding yourself accountable for getting into the situation or relationship, and taking responsibility for getting yourself out of unworkable situations.

It's OK to let them know the impact. Did the gossip let your secret out, leaving you feeling embarrassed? Integrity is owning your part in the matter. Did you share a secret with someone who cannot keep it? Communicate how you feel, but own it. Say how you feel in first person language. I feel betrayed. Embarrassed. Angry. Hurt.

Don't share any more secrets with that person. And don't expect an apology. You may or may not get one.

Another way to hold someone accountable is to take appropriate action. Did you marry an addict? Own your mistake. Decide what your options are, and which one feels appropriate to act on. Leave? Request they get help?

Stage an intervention?

If the other person is unwilling to change, integrity is removing yourself from unworkable and possibly dangerous situations. You can only do so much.

Continue to treat the other person with dignity and respect. Stand in the possibility that they might change, but let go of the expectation that they will change.

The only person you can change is you. Hoping that someone else will change is energy draining.

Trust yourself and act accordingly. Take responsibility for whether or not you keep that person in your life. If you stay, own the consequences.

Don't marry someone who is experiencing addiction and then complain. Don't share secrets with a gossip and then get upset when your secret gets out. Don't hold a promise-breaker to a promise and then be disappointed when the promise isn't kept.

Trust yourself. Trust that you are excellent exactly as you are. Trust is accepting your flaws as well as your strengths. Trust that it's okay to be vulnerable and transparent. Allow people to know where you stand and where your boundaries are.

Trust life. Trust your vision. Trust yourself to handle the Big, Juicy Goals you want to accomplish. Trust gives you power and we all know how sexy powerful people are!

TRUTH

We tend to think of truth as being absolute. It's not.

We once believed that Earth was the center of the Universe and everything revolved around us. Until we knew better. We once believed the earth was flat. Until we knew better. We once believed that illness could be prevented or cured through bloodletting. Until we knew better.

Perhaps in fifty or a hundred years, much of what we believe now will no longer be true. By then, we may know better.

The idea that nothing you think is true might be a tough pill for you to swallow. But there's a ton of freedom in it if you can stomach it.

Don't worry. You won't have to permanently throw away everything you think or believe. You can always take it back.

Letting go of the idea that anything is "true" gives you room to play with a variety of perspectives. Recognizing that what you have is merely a point of view takes the energy out of having to win or fight to be right about what's "true."

Have you accepted any of these as true:

- Someone else's opinion about whether you are smart or dumb, worthy or useless, or who and what you are capable of becoming?
- Someone else's point of view about a particular race, culture, gender preference, or religious belief without investigating whether it's true?
- The media's ideas about beauty and talent?
- Your own opinion about what you deserve or do not deserve?
- That the way you see yourself and the world is accurate?

One aspect of living an awake and alive life is having the ability to let go of what you think you "know." It takes you back to a childlike state of wonder and curiosity.

Children suspend "truth" when they turn a table into a tent, a fort, or a mountain. But they ultimately understand it's a table.

Childlike curiosity gives you the room and freedom to delve into your own truth. Something wonderful happens when you look inside for your truth rather than looking outside of you for validation. Your mind gets quiet. Your whole demeanor grounds itself in wonder and awe.

You can get to that place through many paths: journaling, meditation, exercise, spiritual practices, and asking yourself quality questions. What is beautiful, smart, delicious, and sassy about you? What makes you feel useful, joyful, and fulfilled? What do you find rewarding and worthy of your time, talent, and energy?

It often feels like a holy moment to me when I see clients connect to the beautiful truth of who they are. For me, it's like looking into the eyes of God and experiencing a miracle. Dreams coming from that God-place inside you are powerful, purposeful, and passionate.

You can't help but be moved and inspired to take action on dreams that align with your inner truth. You'll want to play differently, and your play will become lighthearted, childlike, and innocent.

Trust your truth. It will ground you. At the same time, it will be your North Star for creating a meaningful and fulfilling life game.

"T" Remodeling Techniques:

- Pick a "T" word from this chapter as your theme for the day or week. Write it down and keep it with you.

- What resonates with you about this word? Journal or meditate your thoughts.

- Use your "T" word in conversation. Share what it means to you with someone. Ask what it means to them. Write down any insights that open up.

- Take at least one action consistent with the word you chose.

- Does a different "T" word resonate with you? Write it down and do the exercises on this page with the word you chose.

- Make a list of the major transitions or milestones in your life: graduation, marriage, birth of your first child, loss of a job, etc. What was your life like before? How did it change afterward? What did you learn? How did the experience make you stronger?

- Think about an area of your life where you would like to feel more effective and powerful. What do you believe about that area? How do you know it's true? If you let go of that, what else could be true in that area?

U

UNREASONABLE

Gandhi was unreasonable when he talked about getting the British out of India. Nelson Mandela was unreasonable when he talked about ending the practice of apartheid. Kennedy was unreasonable when he declared we would put someone on the moon in ten years.

Worthy things don't get done by reasonable people. They get done by people who see beyond what's reasonable to what's possible.

An acquaintance of mine has taken up the cause of abolishing Genetically Modified Organisms (GMOs). She founded an organization called "Moms Across America." She's traveled the country sharing the impact she believes GMOs have on our health. She's rallying other concerned moms to her cause. Her passion is forwarding a movement that is growing and gaining momentum. That's being unreasonable.

Another friend had a blood transfusion when he was two years old that led to an HIV diagnosis when he was seven. The doctors said he'd be dead by age ten.

For a long time, he waited to die. What was the point of planning a future? In his late teens or early twenties, he decided that since he wasn't dead yet, he ought to do something about creating a future. So he established the "Cameron Siemers Foundation for Hope." Its purpose is to serve young people who have life-threatening illnesses and have lived beyond their life expectancies. Each year, his organization gives grants to young people so they can create projects that make a difference. That's being unreasonable.

In a commencement speech he delivered at the Maharishi University of Management in 2014, Actor Jim Carey said, "We often choose our path based on fear disguised as practicality." What would be possible in your life if you reached beyond what you "know" to be practical and reasonable to explore what's possible? Imagine what you could accomplish.

You don't have to start a movement or create a foundation. All you have to do is choose something that ignites a fire in your belly and go after it with genuine gusto.

UNREASONABLE

Step beyond what you think is reasonable. Make something unreasonable happen that matters to you. It won't take long before you start to feel sexy, vibrant, and fully alive!

UPLIFT

Uplifting others is sexy. People are attracted to people who lift them up.

I recently received a call from a client who was in the midst of an upset, requesting that we meet. She had been invited to a wedding in her home country. She was on the verge of not going because she had so many concerns.

She was concerned about her weight. She was concerned about how the families would feel about her. She was concerned about spending money to go if she was only going to end up being miserable. She was concerned she wouldn't have a good time with people she didn't know.

The committee in her head was dressed in full sabotage gear and on patrol to launch a sneak attack and conquer her joy! Mind you, this woman is a powerful transformational coach who makes a huge difference in the lives of people she coaches. It goes to show how quickly and easily the committee can take control when you stop paying attention.

My role was to help her remember who she really is—a powerful, funny, intelligent, strong woman. Watching her as we talked was almost like watching someone wake up from a bad dream.

She went from looking old and tired to looking bright and bubbly. She began to smile and laugh as she brought herself out of her anxiety and into the present moment.

When she was able to hush the committee up long enough to hear the voice of her heart, she realized that she was capable of having a great time and bringing joy to others. Her excitement about attending the wedding returned and she decided to go, after all.

When she got back, she called to tell me what a wonderful time she had partying, dancing, and interacting with everyone. She had created an intention to be an instigator of fun. She felt she had been successful at being an uplifting presence at the wedding. She came home feeling happy and rested.

How do you think my client would have felt had she stayed home and missed out on the wedding? How many people do you think were uplifted by her exuberant and joyful presence? And all she had to do was show up and be her genuine, sparkly, sexy self!

And you had better believe I was uplifted when I heard what a wonderful time she had on her trip. I couldn't help but smile!

With every interaction, you have a choice to disparage or uplift another human being. Next time you want to add negative energy to an interaction, take a time out. Look to see if you are the one in need of uplifting. If so, there are sexier ways for you to feel better about yourself than by putting someone else down. It may be as simple as:

- Asking for support, as my client did.
- Getting curious about what it would take for you to feel so good you don't feel the need to belittle anyone else. Ever. For any reason.
- Giving away what you want. You will be uplifted when you uplift others.

When you uplift one person, you are raising both your energy vibration and theirs. In his 2004 book *The Power of Intention,* Wayne Dyer says that you only need to raise your personal vibration level slightly to have an impact on the vibrational energy of the planet. By regularly practicing kindness and love, seeing beauty and the good in yourself and others, you will uplift the negative energy of 90,000 people living in low energy vibrations like hate, guilt, and anger.

If two people practice love, peace, kindness and joy, the impact isn't 90,000 plus 90,000, it's 90,000 times 90,000. Think of the impact that hundreds or thousands of us could have! What could be more powerful or sexy than that?

We are each capable of doing it and it doesn't take much effort. A kind word. A gesture of support. Listening with full and nonjudgmental attention. Contacting someone you know and sharing what they said or did that uplifted you. Authentically apologizing to someone you've hurt. Sharing bread pudding and whiskey sauce or hugs and laughter with a friend.

Give it a try. Practice uplifting someone else any time you feel in need of uplifting. Take note of how your energy shifts.

"U" Remodeling Techniques:

- Pick a "U" word from this chapter as your theme for the day or week. Write it down and keep it with you.

- What resonates with you about this word? Journal or meditate your thoughts.

- Use your "U" word in conversation. Share what it means to you with someone. Ask what it means to them. Write down any insights that open up.

- Take at least one action consistent with the word you chose.

- Does a different "U" word resonate with you? Write it down and do the exercises on this page with the word you chose.

- Pick an area of your life where joy, freedom or ease is missing and you are behaving reasonably or "tolerating" something. What would it take for you to be unreasonable with yourself or someone else in that area?

- Contact someone you know and practice having an uplifting conversation. Notice if the conversation takes on a negative tone, such as complaining or gossip. Practice steering the conversation in a more powerful and uplifting direction. Notice how you felt before and after the conversation.

V

VALUES

For much of my life, I didn't know how to answer questions about what I value. I'd mumble some silly robot answer about valuing my job or my friends or my family.

You are "supposed" to value those things, right? And of course, I do. But I never stopped to question what I'd been taught. If asked, I couldn't say specifically what mattered to me about my job, friendships, family, or anything else.

My eyes were opened a few years ago when I took a behavior style assessment. I had done Myers-Briggs years ago, and it was great. But the values portion of this particular behavior style assessment rocked my world.

Based on your answers, it ranks seven values from highest to lowest. The two values that score the highest represent what matters most to you at this point in your life.

Seeing my top two values was eye opening. As I thought about them, I could look back over my career and see why I performed better and had more fun on particular projects and assignments than I did on others. I could see why certain projects and assignments were energy draining and grueling for me.

The fun projects aligned closely with my values. The energy-draining, grueling projects did not.

Knowing your "why" for doing what you do is powerful. Clarity about my values gave me the confidence I needed to help me design my Sexy Second Act as a career and life design coach.

I now offer behavior style assessments to my clients. Sometimes it confirms they are on the right path. It often helps them understand where adjustments are required that will align them more closely with what matters to them. That alignment helps them move forward quickly to design and build a Sexy Second Act they are excited about. Excitement tones down the committee's resistance and allows imagination and creativity to show up.

Doesn't it make sense that it's easier and more fun to design a Sexy Second

VALUES

Act that aligns with your values? A paycheck ought to be about more than dollars and cents.

Values represent emotions. For example, you may say you value money, but there's a deeper emotion behind it that represents what money means to you, like freedom, security, the ability to provide for your loved ones, or contribute to causes in a meaningful way.

Let's say your top two values are money (economic) and beauty (aesthetic). At first, you might see that as a clash of values. If you dig deeper into how to put these values together, you might hit upon an elegant way to make money that makes things beautiful. Flipping houses. Landscape design. Ecological vacation experiences. The possibilities are endless based on your unique skills, what you love doing, and where you would like to make a difference.

You become energized when you design your Sexy Second Act around what you value. High energy allows you to bring your imagination, creativity, and curiosity to what you do. It pulls you through on days when the going gets rough. Values act as a compass to get you back on course if you get sidetracked.

If you are struggling to figure out how to create meaning in the second half of your life, play with possibilities for what your values are. What do you love to do? What do you love about that? What makes you forget about time when you do them? What makes you forget about yourself?

Your friends and colleagues can help, too. Ask them to describe you in a word or short phrase. If you often hear the same word or phrase, it might be a key to unlocking something you value. Do they say you are loyal? Fun-loving? Generous? Free-spirited? Kind-hearted?

Are there words in this book that resonate with you? Explore whether one or more of them reflect your values. Play with ways you can use your values in your Sexy Second Act life or career design.

VIBRATION

I used to be skeptical about the idea of vibrational energy when it came to manifesting what you want. Looking back, that seems a little crazy, considering that the universe appears to be made up of energy that is constantly in motion and changing form.

Reading a wonderful book called *Power vs. Force* by David Hawkins changed my mind. Using muscle testing, he studied vibrational energy and created a scale that measures levels of human consciousness from low-vibration shadow energy to high-vibration enlightened energy. The scale ranges from 20, the shadow energy of shame, to 1000, the energy of enlightenment.

As a planet, humans have a long way to go before we reach the energy vibration of enlightenment. The theory goes that only avatars such as Jesus, Buddha, and Krishna vibrate at that level.

On the Hawkins scale, 200 marks where we cross over the line from the shadow into the light. The first energy after crossing the line is "courage." That makes sense. You need courage to consciously make anything happen.

When the book was written, he said human consciousness is emerging from the shadow for the first time. At that time, we had reached an energy vibration level of roughly 204 on his scale.

I recently read an article claiming that human consciousness is currently vibrating at about 207. That still falls within the range of courage, but it shows we are making progress on the road to becoming enlightened.

Vibrations below 200 are energy drainers. Vibrations above 200 are energy enhancers. Below 200, you are sucking more energy than you are contributing. Above 200, you are contributing more energy than you are taking.

What is your primary energy vibration? If you usually feel angry, sad, depressed, or ashamed, you are primarily vibrating in shadow energy. If you usually feel courageous, joyful, accepting or loving, you are primarily vibrating in light energy.

How do you raise your vibrational energy? Laugh, do something you love, dance, play your favorite sport, or share a celebration moment. It could even be as simple as sharing bread pudding and whiskey sauce with a friend and enjoying every bite.

The scale offers an intriguing and thought-provoking theory. We often think it takes huge sacrifices to make a difference when all that's necessary is for each of us to perform acts of kindness, peacefulness, joy, love, or compassion.

Under that theory, you have an opportunity to create an interesting and sexy life game. All it takes is for you to commit your life to something that serves others and brings you authentic happiness and fulfillment.

Save yourself and you save the planet. What's the worst that could happen if you gave living your life according to that philosophy a shot?

VIVID VISION

When you design an intention, you start moving energy. When you translate your intention into a vivid vision, you build momentum. Building momentum keeps the committee in your head from killing your dreams.

A vivid vision is a specific picture of how you want your intention to show up in reality. Winning Olympic athletes often describe in rich detail how they vividly pictured every step or stroke of their winning events. It's uncanny how their victories unfold exactly as they envisioned them.

So how come visioning works successfully for some people and not for others? Effective visioning paints a picture in your brain. When you see that picture, your brain cannot tell the difference between it and reality.

Your body reacts and "vibrates" to the energy of the picture you have painted. When you vision effectively, you've got to feel the juice! By itself, thinking won't turn your vision into reality. It's like putting the cart before the horse.

Picture yourself biting into a juicy, tart lemon. If you vision effectively, your mouth starts to water. Your brain can't tell you aren't actually biting into a lemon.

Your body reacts the same way to your vivid vision. You'll feel excitement, joy or anticipation.

Whether you are vividly visioning your dream job, dream vacation, or excellent relationship, bring all your five senses into it. How do you feel? How does your dream look, taste, smell, and sound? Who is with you? What are you doing? Where are you doing it?

Adding props to your vivid vision supports you even further to bring your vision into reality. Be as creative as you want. Here are a few examples:

- Write your vivid vision and read it aloud daily … with feeling!
- Record your vivid vision on audio and play it back before falling asleep.
- Create vision boards displaying pictures and phrases that represent what you want.

- Create a 3-D image. One friend made a construction paper model of a building. Each room represented an area of her life, such as health, family, finances or relationships. She placed a token in each room for what she wanted to manifest in that area.
- Create a short video and watch it daily.
- Surround yourself with props that reflect your vision. If you want to travel to a specific place, get a poster. One client wanted to buff up, so he hung a poster of an athletic role-model on the back of his office door. He added inspiring quotes to remind him of his goal and keep him on track.

Staying in touch with your vivid vision gives the committee in your head a new job. It has to go to work on how to deliver your vision to you. It will help you generate new ideas. Ideas generate excitement. Excitement leads you to take action. Action leads to victory!

For another layer of accountability and support, share your vivid vision with trusted friends and associates, get coaching, or join a mastermind group. Your dream becomes real when it's alive in another person who can offer ideas and resources you haven't thought of.

The practice of vivid visioning boosts your life force energy. It keeps you in action even on tough days when nothing seems to be working.

Regular vivid visioning keeps you feeling electric, juicy, and powerful. Your dreams will happen! When you achieve success on turning your vivid vision into reality, you'll feel vibrant, alive, and sexy!

"V" Remodeling Techniques:

- Pick a "V" word from this chapter as your theme for the day or week. Write it down and keep it with you.

- What resonates with you about this word? Journal or meditate your thoughts.

- Use your "V" word in conversation. Share what it means to you with someone. Ask what it means to them. Write down any insights that open up.

- Take at least one action consistent with the word you chose.

- Does a different "V" word resonate with you? Write it down and do the exercises on this page with the word you chose.

- Take your "energy temperature" several times a day. Notice whether you are operating in the shadow or in the light. Take an action that will raise your energy temperature. Forgive. Have gratitude. Laugh. Hug someone you care about. Notice how you feel afterward.

- Create a vivid vision for at least one area of your life. Write it down or use props to immerse yourself in your vision. If you feel the urge to take an action, take it even if it doesn't make sense. Notice any outcomes or acts of serendipity that occur.

W

WHO

Who are your "whos"? To create a bodaciously badass Sexy Second Act, it's important to know who is on your "who roster." Think about:

- Who acknowledges you?
- Who never bullshits you?
- Who is committed to your success?
- Who dances with you?
- Who embraces you?
- Who is fierce for you?
- Who helps you grow?
- Who supports your hustle?
- Who has integrity?
- Who shares your joy?
- Who helps you K.I.S.S.?
- Who listens to you?
- Who masterminds with you?
- Who's brave enough to say "no" to you?
- Who plays with you?
- Who asks you quality questions?
- Who is rigorous with you?
- Who keeps you feelin' sexy?
- Whom do you trust?
- Who uplifts you?
- Who has values you admire?
- Whom do you rely on for wisdom?
- Who gives you X-ray clarity?
- With whom do you share yum?
- Who helps you find your zone?

Jumping into a Big, Juicy Goal or life game is scary and feels super-hard if you think you have to do it by yourself. Don't fall into the typically American trap of believing in the lone hero who dashes in to save the day and then rides off into the sunset alone.

When you look closer, you'll see that very few heroes truly go it alone. They often have a sidekick. Or else someone with a stake in the outcome shows up to help. The Lone Ranger had Tonto, but the townspeople often stepped in at the last minute to help. They had a stake in the outcome. What stakeholders need is a powerful leader to help them see victory is possible.

It's OK to include people you don't know on your "who roster." Look for role models doing what you want to do.

Read their books and blogs. Take their workshops. Follow them online. And if they provide you with something that takes you or your life or career to a new level, drop them a note and thank them. They'd love the acknowledgement and hearing how they made a difference for you.

Whose "who roster" are you on? To whom are you offering your wisdom and talents?

That's important. By helping and supporting others, you'll have a wealth of people to add to your "who roster" who will be excited to support you should the need arise. Everyone generates more energy, adding to the fun and excitement.

WISDOM

I don't care how old or young you are, you have a wealth of wisdom inside you. You may not know it. You may not have demonstrated it in your life so far, but it's there. You may just have forgotten how to access it or you may not know how to trust it.

I've seen brilliant eighteen-year-olds wisely coach equally brilliant and feisty forty-, fifty-, and sixty-somethings, leading them to breakthroughs that changed their lives. I've seen fifty- and sixty-somethings coach know-it-all twenty-somethings with compassion, patience and love that resulted in lifelong friendships.

Don Miguel Ruiz and Don Jose Ruiz with Janet Mills wrote in their 2010 book, *The Fifth Agreement: A Practical Guide to Self-Mastery*, that we should "be skeptical, but learn to listen." To me, that's the essence of wisdom. That means not only listening to what others tell you, it's tuning in to your own intuition, learning to listen to what it tells you, and not blowing it off if it disagrees with something that's going on outside of you.

One of my clients is learning to recognize, tap into, and trust her inner wisdom. She's in the midst of designing her Sexy Second Act. In the meantime, she is looking for a career opportunity that will bring her an income and help her round out her skills.

She got her former job on a recommendation and never had to prepare a resume. Tackling that chore has escalated her anxiety level to DEFCON 4. The committee in her head is telling her she hasn't done anything worth putting on a resume.

We started with a behavior style assessment to help her uncover what she liked and didn't like about her former job. As we reviewed it, she suddenly burst out, "I don't want to do the detail work; I want to be the conductor!" meaning she loves bringing the right resources together to solve problems.

Bingo! She knew it somewhere inside all along. The committee kept her from accessing her inner wisdom until she started talking about what she's good at and what she wants. She now has a starting place for pulling together events for her resume where she demonstrated her ability to be a conductor.

Good coaching helps you get in touch with your own inner wisdom. But you can coach yourself to become what my friend Kathy calls a "self-cleaning oven."

Meditating, journaling, asking quality questions, vivid visioning, reading, and listening to talks from people you look up to and admire are great ways to help you tap into your inner wisdom.

Pay attention to what resonates with you. Your body knows. Pay attention when you feel like something or someone is "off." Pay attention when you feel excited or curious. Follow the thread. You'll love where your own inner wisdom takes you.

"W" Remodeling Techniques:

- Pick a "W" word from this chapter as your theme for the day or week. Write it down and keep it with you.

- What resonates with you about this word? Journal or meditate your thoughts.

- Use your "W" word in conversation. Share what it means to you with someone. Ask what it means to them. Write down any insights that open up.

- Take at least one action consistent with the word you chose.

- Does a different "W" word resonate with you? Write it down and do the exercises on this page with the word you chose.

- Make two "who" lists; one list for who supports you and a second for who you can help and support. Who has knowledge, resources, and skills that can support you as you begin designing your Sexy Second Act? Who can you support with your skills, knowledge and talents? Make appointments to call or meet with them. Have conversations about how you might support each other.

- Think about times when you have listened to your inner wisdom and times when you ignored it. What happened? What lessons did you learn? What practices will you put into place to help you pay attention to your inner wisdom?

X

X-RAY VISION

We take many modern miracles for granted. X-rays are one of them. Can you imagine how magical and exciting it must have been to see the very first X-rays ever taken?

For the first time, we could visually explore the previously unseen world of our bodies and how they work. It's incredible that medical professionals can look beneath the surface of your skin to pinpoint the source of possible problems in your body and treat them.

There's a wonderful commercial about diversity produced in 2015 by the Ad Council. It's called "Love Has No Labels." It starts with a variety of people standing behind an X-ray machine. All you see is their skeletons moving.

It's only when they come out from behind the screen that you see their diversity. Young, old, gay, straight, friends, neighbors, family members, and various ethnic and religious identities.

X-rays tell the truth. The truth that underneath the surface, we are all the same. The rest is what we make up.

I once invited two women friends of mine to lunch. They were from different Middle-Eastern countries and I wanted them to meet. I thought they might become friends. Listening to their conversation gave me a fascinating glimpse into the world of perception.

One lady is a powerhouse in her career. She has overcome many obstacles in a male-dominated field to achieve an executive-level position.

The other lady, equally intelligent and talented, was stalled in her career. She had many complaints about being a woman and how unfairly women are treated. She couldn't believe it when she learned that the other woman had risen to an executive position without having been harassed in one way or another.

I loved how the executive replied. She said, "I don't even think about that happening. It's just not an issue for me."

Two intelligent women with two very different perceptions. Two very different life experiences. What they believed on the inside showed up on the outside.

X-ray visioning is the practical side of dreaming. You can be your own X-ray machine by being willing to look beneath the surface to see the difference between what's true and what we make up. You may be shocked to learn how little is real.

Be willing to X-ray the underside, inside, and outside of everything you believe. Jettison anything that blocks you from becoming your healthiest, highest and best self, living joyfully and congruently. Jettison anything that blocks you from the experience of love. Jettison anything that blocks you from your connection to others.

Gospel and jazz singer Ethel Waters said, "God don't sponsor no flops." If that's true, then no matter who you are or where you come from, you deserve all the good the Universe has in store for you. It's a great quote to remember when the committee tells you that some people matter more than other people, or that you matter less or are less deserving than anyone else.

Use your X-ray vision to look past what you see and "know" on the surface. What you see underneath may surprise you. Beneath the wounds we all have; beneath the armor we put on to protect ourselves; beneath what we make up about each other and ourselves; is a human being doing the best he or she can do.

You never know. When you look beneath the surface, the person you have judged, misjudged, or avoided getting to know, may be your next best friend, the love you've been looking for, or the colleague who can help you take your career or life to the next level.

"X" Remodeling Techniques:

- Pick an "X" word from this chapter as your theme for the day or week. Write it down and keep it with you.

- What resonates with you about this word? Journal or meditate your thoughts.

- Use your "X" word in conversation. Share what it means to you with someone. Ask them what it means to them. Write down any insights that open up.

- Take at least one action consistent with the word you chose.

- Does a different "X" word resonate with you? Write it down and do the exercises on this page with the word you chose.

- What belief or relationship are you willing to X-ray to get to the truth of where love and connection are missing? What action are you willing to take to restore love and connection?

Y

YEAR

The beginning of a new year, whether it's January 1, Chinese New Year, your birthday, or some other milestone of your choosing, represents a fabulous opportunity to take a time out and reflect on your previous year. Start by asking yourself quality questions. What did you do that worked? What did you do that didn't work? What accomplishments do you want to celebrate? What lessons did you learn? What new skill did you master?

Once you've reflected on the past year, you can focus on the upcoming year. What would you like to accomplish? What would you most like to learn? What would you most like to unlearn? What would you like to do this year that will matter most in five years?

For extra momentum, you can take it one step further and create a yearly theme. One year mine was "lighthearted laser focus." I created my goals for the year based on that theme.

Pick a song that aligns with your theme. Listen to it every time you need an energy boost. One of my favorites is "That Power" by Will.i.am, featuring Justin Bieber. When I need a boost, I play that song in my head. I feel an instant shift in my body when I make the moves they make in the video.

The point is to set your year up to be fun and productive. Creating a theme can help you develop goals that align with it. It makes goal setting more fun than setting them the way we traditionally do. Setting goals in the "traditional" way mostly leads to what I call "Resolution Resignation.™"

One way to set fun goals is to eliminate any goal that has a "should" in front of it. Goals like these:

- I "should" lose weight.
- I "should" quit my job.
- I "should" quit smoking.

Setting "should" goals is fodder for the committee to jump in and start giving you a bunch of nay-saying blah-blah-blah, like, "How often have you tried that?" "It hasn't worked so far." "What makes you think it's going to work this time?" "Give it up and go order a pizza."

"Should" goals set you up for failure. By the end of January, gyms are empty, you are still dragging yourself to a job you hate, and you are thinking that standing outside to smoke when it's 40° F below isn't so bad after all. Resolution Resignation™ has set in.

It's all in the way you frame it. Wouldn't it be fun to set goals in a way that excites, delights, and inspires you? Start with what you want, like these examples:

- a body that's fit, flexible, fabulous and flirty … or studly
- to live and work on an island in my swimsuit and take people on ocean play adventures
- to work for a great company where I am paid well, feel valued, and my contribution makes a difference.

Goals come naturally when you get clear about what you want. Don't these examples sound sexier and more fun to pursue? How would your year go differently if you set your goals up this way?

The more exciting and fun you make your goals, the more likely you are to accomplish them. And just think how much fun your year will be.

YOLO — YOU ONLY LIVE ONCE

You only live once. At least as far as we know. When you think about that, doesn't it seem nuts to spend your precious time doing things that make no sense? Things such as:

- commuting several hours each way to a job you hate?
- being married to someone who is unwilling or unable to honor and care for you?
- staying in toxic friendships filled with gossip where you worry about how you measure up to some bogus ideal about how you should live your life?

You may call yourself a businessperson, doctor, truck driver, banker, housewife, artist, real estate agent or CEO. That's what you do. It isn't who you are.

You are not flat like a piece of glass. You are a sparkling diamond with many facets you can spend a lifetime exploring.

The bad news is that you can no longer depend on anything that used to represent stability. The good news is that you have marvelous gifts inside you that you have yet to tap into. The other good news is that we have reached a time in our evolution where it's easier than ever to find ways to do so.

Yes, it will require you to look at the world like a renegade. It will require you to look at ways to earn a living in ways you've never done. And you may have to update your skills by including education and training in your planning.

But if you only live once, isn't it time to organize your priorities in such a way that when it comes time for you to kiss this life goodbye, you can do so with a sense of peace rather than regret? Steve Jobs said it best in his 2005 commencement address at Stanford:

"I have looked in the mirror every morning and asked myself: 'If today were the last day of my life, would I want to do what I am about to do today?'

And whenever the answer has been 'No' for too many days in a row, I know I need to change something."

If today was the last day of your life, would you be doing what you are about to do today? You don't have to do a complete about-face. A shift of one degree is enough to alter your life. One change is all it takes. What small change can you make today that will head you in the direction of your Sexy Second Act?

YUM

Yum is a word that's downright fun. You can't mistake it for being anything other than out-and-out delicious.

A colleague declared that he wanted his life to be about the "feeling of yum." You could see sparkle and mischief in his eyes when he announced it. How sexy do you think his life will become by making the feeling of yum his organizing principle for designing and building health, relationships, wealth, relaxation time, and a great career, or business?

That doesn't mean every second of every day feels yummy. Life doesn't work that way.

What it does mean is that he has a compass for moving consistently in that direction. It gives him guidance for saying "no" to opportunities that don't align with the feeling of yum, and "yes" to opportunities that do.

Choices become simple, certain, and elegant. He has a stake in the ground for envisioning what he wants and designing Big, Juicy Goals accordingly.

As a leader, his example can inspire others to step into their own yumminess. And the more of us who are willing to move in that direction, the sweeter life is for all of us.

I'll never forget a story I once read about a father who stood admiring a sunset with his grown daughter. The daughter was going through a hard time. She complained to her father that if you added up all the beautiful moments in life, they probably wouldn't total much more than an hour. The father turned, gazed into her eyes and replied softly, "Yes. Precious, aren't they?"

Make a practice of noticing the yummy moments in your life. Kids' hugs. Puppies. Warm feet by the fire. Hot chocolate. A soft blanket and a good book. Snuggles with your sweetie. Special moments you share with your partner. Toes in the sand.

Savor the yum with gratitude when it shows up. And who knows? You might double, or even triple, the amount of yum in your life! How sexy would that be?

"Y" Remodeling Techniques:

- Pick a "Y" word from this chapter as your theme for the day or week. Write it down and keep it with you.

- What resonates with you about this word? Journal or meditate your thoughts.

- Use your "Y" word in conversation. Share what it means to you with someone. Ask them to share what it means to them. Write down any insights that open up.

- Take at least one action consistent with the word you chose.

- Does a different "Y" word resonate with you? Write it down and do the exercises on this page with the word you chose.

- Pick a theme for your year. Make it a word or phrase you can use as a basis for setting your goals.

- Make a list of the yummy moments you've experienced in your life. What made them yummy? What other yummy moments would you like to experience? What actions can you take to make them happen?

Z

ZERO

Zero is a cool, flexible, interesting number. Starting from zero indicates new beginnings. Ending with zero indicates completion. Zero in the middle is a placeholder that makes its surrounding numbers more important.

Zero is a humble number that maintains its equilibrium wherever it's placed. It doesn't brag, it just does its job. There's a grand lesson in that.

When people feel like they are a "zero," or call someone else a "zero," they don't generally mean it as a compliment. I think they are way off base. Zero cannot be something you are; it can only be a location. A beginning. An end. Or a middle.

Zero at the end may be a place where you feel like everything you had or knew is gone. It may be the result of a misfortune. It may be the result of poor choices.

You may feel like there's nothing left and nowhere to go from there. The committee will do its best to convince you that's true. It will try to convince you that's who you are, not where you are.

We often refer to the place where everything that previously existed and now is lost as Ground Zero. When you first look at it, it appears that zero is the end. There is work to do. It's called grieving. Grieving helps you complete the past, so that you can begin again with peace and hope.

Grieving is a process that takes as long as it takes. This is where zero in the middle comes in. Zero in the middle gives you the space to work your way through what you need to work through to complete something and prepare for a new beginning. On the surface, it may look like nothing is happening, but a lot of work is going on underneath.

Zero in the middle is where you listen to your heart and your Higher Power. From that still place, you have the opportunity to find a way to move forward, one step at a time. When you find that path, zero once again becomes the start of a new beginning.

If you have reached Ground Zero in your life and you are still on the planet, I acknowledge you. I honor you. I celebrate you. You have something precious that not everyone has. You have courage and you have grit. The only other thing you need is a compelling dream.

Courage, grit, and a dream are invaluable tools for jump-starting your journey from Ground Zero to Hero. Use them to raise yourself up. Build a bodaciously badass Sexy Second Act that's magnificent, strong, and beautiful.

ZIGZAG

When I was enrolled in community college, I took a class where we were given an assignment to interview someone we admired and respected. I chose to interview my dad.

Several of his answers surprised me during that interview, but the one I remember most was his response when I asked if he had any regrets. He said he didn't. He believed he'd lived a pretty good life.

His answer took me aback because almost nothing in his life worked out the way he wanted it to. He had not had an easy upbringing. There had been turmoil in his relationship with his father. The Depression and World War II sabotaged his opportunity to finish college. He and my mom had a difficult marriage.

Despite the zigzags, he never became bitter. He always saw life as good. He seemed to know how to make the best of whatever circumstances came his way. In that sense, he is my biggest role model.

We start out early in life naively wanting it to go in a straightforward, upward direction. We get disappointed and think it's unfair when things don't go our way.

Danish philosopher Soren Kierkegaard said that life must be lived forward, but can only be understood backward. When we look back, life's zigzags are often the best parts, even though it doesn't feel that way when we are in the middle of one. It can feel like we aren't going anywhere; but in hindsight, we can see that zigzags do show forward movement. Sometimes it's with baby steps and sometimes we take a quantum leap.

Either way, you learned. You stretched. You survived. You came through the zigzags stronger and wiser. So embrace the zigzags of your life. They may be the most important parts of being here in Earth school.

"Z" Remodeling Techniques:

- Pick a "Z" word from this chapter as your theme for the day or week. Write it down and keep it with you.

- What resonates with you about this word? Journal or meditate your thoughts.

- Use your "Z" word in conversation. Share what it means to you with someone. Ask what it means to them. Write down any insights that open up.

- Take at least one action consistent with the word you chose.

- Does a different "Z" word resonate with you? Write it down and do the exercises on this page with the word you chose.

- What are the biggest lessons you've learned from your Ground Zero moments? How can you put them to use as part of your Sexy Second Act?

Final Thoughts

Congratulations! You've made it to the end of the book. Here we are, back to zero.

If you've stuck with me and completed the exercises, my hat is off to you! You are a champion and a hero for coming this far!

The ending of this book is your beginning. Take what you've discovered here and use it to do something exciting. Sexy is about living your life playfully and with passion, doing something meaningful with the rest of your life, and remembering that a paycheck is as much about fulfilling your legacy as it is about the money.

Embrace the divine insanity it is to be human. Laugh out loud when things get crazy. But keep going. Design and live your Sexy Second Act. The world needs you to lead the way with your commitment and your courage.

I'd love to hear the progress you are making and what kind of Sexy Second Act you are designing. I'd love to celebrate your remodeling milestones.

My favorite Irish blessing expresses my intention and wish for you as we end our journey together:

May your joys be as bright as the morning,
And your sorrows merely be shadows that fade,
In the sunlight of love.

May you have enough happiness to keep you sweet.
Enough trials to keep you strong.
Enough sorrows to keep you human.
Enough hope to keep you happy.
Enough failure to keep you humble.
Enough success to keep you eager.
Enough friends to give you comfort.
Enough faith and courage in yourself to banish sadness.
Enough wealth to meet your needs.

And one thing more: enough determination to make each day a more wonderful day than the day before.

Author Biography

Sue's coaching career was launched as a result of her personal journey through a mid-life career transition. This experience launched her desire to help clients design richly fulfilling "Sexy, Second Act Careers" that combine Passion, Purpose, and a Paycheck!®

Her mission is to help her clients face any career or life transition with curiosity, courage, and confidence. Using a variety of personalized tools, assessments and techniques, she guides her clients to discover their own paths leading to integrated and deeply fulfilling lives. She helps her clients in the following ways:

- Discover what they are passionate about
- Design an empowering job fit strategy that aligns with their passions
- Develop a sense of personal entrepreneurship and career ownership
- Rediscover joy and meaning in their professional and personal lives
- See new possibilities for designing a Sexy Second Act Career and Life that includes Passion, Purpose and a Paycheck!®

Sue's clients say she has the capacity to believe in their dreams for them until they can do so on their own. Through training, solid experience, curiosity, and a genuine love for people, Sue has developed a compassionate and fun-loving approach to help clients transition into independent, flexible, and rewarding "Sexy Second Act Careers".

Sue's "Sexy Second Act" career was launched as the result of a corporate down-sizing. She's faced what her clients are facing. She is the poster child for what many people, especially Baby Boomers, are doing to create new careers that combine Passion, Purpose, and a Paycheck®.

She discovered coaching through participation in a personal growth seminar. Working with a coach helped her successfully navigate her career transition to found the business she loves where she is passionate about helping others to remodel their careers and lives.

Her background includes a successful and rewarding career in project and training management. Three Squares Coaching and Consulting was created out of her personal journey. Her experience, combined with an extensive coaching background, gives her an in-depth insight into how her clients can face any career or life transition with curiosity, courage, and confidence.

Sue's qualifications include the following:

- Professional Behavior Style Analyst
- Certified Behavior Assessment Coach
- Certified Strategy and Accountability Coach
- 30+ years of corporate experience in Training and Project Management
- 10+ years as a Career and Life Design Coach

Designing Your Sexy Second Act? Let's mastermind and share ideas.

In Think and Grow Rich, Napoleon Hill said that no individual may have great power without availing himself of the "Master Mind," which is created by blending, in a spirit of perfect harmony, two or more minds. From this blending arises a more powerful "third mind," that amps up the power of the entire group, much like a group of batteries generates more energy than a single battery.

Here are some ways to powerfully share your ideas and get feedback and support:

1. Visit my website at www.3squarescoaching.com. You'll see possibilities for how you can continue your journey to design and build a Sexy Second Act through workshops, mastermind groups, and private coaching.
2. Please feel free to email me at sue@threesquarescoaching.com. Your ideas and courageous stories about how you are designing and building your Sexy Second Act inspire me!
3. Invite me to speak

Other ways to connect and stay in communication:

BLOG
www.3squarescoaching.com/category/career-training/
TWITTER:
@freshstartcoach
PINTEREST:
www.pinterest.com/coachsue/
FACEBOOK:
www.facebook.com/Sexy.Second.Act/
LINKEDIN:
www.linkedin.com/in/threesquarescoaching

www.ingramcontent.com/pod-product-compliance
Lightning Source LLC
Chambersburg PA
CBHW052133010526
44113CB00035B/2042